Collage of a Life

'It was the best of times, it was the worst of times, it was the age of wisdom, it was the age of foolishness…'
            Charles Dickens, *A Tale of Two Cities*

'I would like, if I may, to take you on a strange journey…'
         Richard O'Brien, *The Rocky Horror Show*

'Come hither'

Collage of a Life

Memoirs of an artist, actor and humorist

Jonathan Adams

Foreword by Timothy West

Silver Link Publishing Ltd

To Joan

© Jonathan Adams and Joan Elliott

All rights reserved. No part of this publication may be reproduced, stored in a retrieval system or transmitted, in any form or by any means, electronic, mechanical, photocopying, recording or otherwise, without prior permission in writing from Silver Link Publishing Ltd.

First published in 2008

British Library Cataloguing in Publication Data

A catalogue record for this book is available from the British Library.

ISBN 978 1 85794 302 3

Silver Link Publishing Ltd
The Trundle
Ringstead Road
Great Addington
Kettering
Northants NN14 4BW

Tel/Fax: 01536 330588
email: sales@nostalgiacollection.com
Website: www.nostalgiacollection.com

The cartoons in the text are by Jonathan Adams

Printed and bound in the Czech Republic

Contents

Acknowledgements 6
Foreword by Timothy West 7
Foreword by Joy Blakeman 9
Preface 11

1 Althorpe 13
2 Family 17
3 War 32
4 School days 37
5 Art School 54
6 The Wicked City 69
7 National Service 85
8 Back to school 101
9 Acting 114

Epilogue 142
Postscript 143

Acknowledgements

'I'd like to thank you but I won't.' (Jonathan Adams)

'I cannot thank you enough.' (Joan Elliott)

I would like to thank the following people: Anthony Garrick and Nigel Lambert, for rostrum camera and art photography; Sally Owen and Don Owen, for graphic design and computer assistance; John Bruce, for art cataloguing; Joy Blakeman, for reading and advising on the original manuscript; Diana Tyler, for legal advice; Tom Lehrer, Sidney Livingstone and *The Hendon Times*, for permission to use words and photographs; Prunella Scales, for her enthusiasm and encouragement to publish; and all those who wrote such kind words of Jonathan.

I would especially like to Timothy West for his thoughtful and entertaining Foreword, and Will Adams and Mick Sanders of Silver Link Publishing Ltd for helping to make it possible.

Joan Elliott

Foreword
by
Timothy West

Reading this entertaining book is like being allowed to peer through a child's kaleidoscope while all the time it is being shaken, struck violently or dropped in tomato soup. The author calls it a collage, and as a remarkable exponent of that particular art form, he ought to know.

At Northampton School of Art, Jonathan eschewed the conservatism of its basic training in favour of Surrealism and Dada; and when he moved up the scale to Chelsea, he felt he'd established himself in the area as 'a minor clownish cult figure'. He admired Max Ernst, Magritte and Salvador Dali among others, and later raided the unsuspecting twilight obscurity of a clutch of English surrealists living in retirement on the South Coast. He had a particular affection for Kurt Schwitters – artist, poet, comedian and collagist extraordinary – and indeed gave a street performance of Schwitters's *Ur Sonata* – 'lanke tr q' pe pe pe pe pe…' – outside the poet's erstwhile dwelling in Chesterfield Road, Barnes.

This book, in a series of vignettes, reveals Jonathan as the polymath that he was – not an attribute he would have thought worthy of comment, much less of pride. While doing his National Service in the RAF in Malaya as a medical orderly, he wrote: 'Washing the fire-extinguisher foam off a dead body; my head was crammed full of all kinds of things – acting – piano playing – singing – painting – writing – I want to do everything; but, as they say, "jack of all trades"…'

I had not read anything of Jonathan's, I think, until Joan gave me a copy of this book. Of his work as a painter/draughtsman/collagist I became fully aware only after we had already been acquainted some 30 years as fellow actors. We used to broadcast together in the old free-wheeling radio days of *Saturday Night Theatre* and the BBC Drama Rep, and later we were together in a stage play called *Master Class*, where Jonathan, playing Stalin's brutish Controller of Arts, suddenly sat down at the grand piano and, to everyone's astonishment, gave a most delicate performance of a Chopin Polonaise. Typically, the image that Jonathan remembered of my own performance in that play was the night my extravagant Stalin moustache came off in mid-scene, and had to be dropped out of sight into the samovar.

The thespian instinct for Jonathan had never lain far below the surface: comic-strip-inspired playlets delivered in the corner of the school playground at break-time, performances with the amateur Northampton Players, songs-at-the-piano at local functions, and entering the religious fundamentalist Carol Levis's travelling talent show with the perhaps unwisely chosen 'Stompin' at the Graveyard Ball'.

Not deterred by this, nor by attempting to play 'Rockin' to Little Mo Muffet' to an audience of inebriated Gordon Highlanders at the Nuffield Centre in Trafalgar Square, Jonathan decided at the age of 28 to leave off teaching art, and become a professional actor. He started slowly. An impressive, big-boned chap, with a face that his Paddington landlady described as that of a drowned Norwegian sailor, this was not the conventional physique required of romantic juveniles – at least, not in the 1960s. Later, of course, that sort of puzzled, slightly resentful mien, that suggestion of a dangerous, eccentric reserve of energy, has become much valued by casting directors and the like, and Tom Lehrer in 1980, after warmly thanking Jonathan for his performance in his show *Tomfoolery*, wrote that 'it has been a pleasure watching your demonstrations of gentle insanity'.

Slow, uncertain progress towards one's goal makes for better reading than meteoric rise. After being waylaid by memories (dear to me because we both worked for him) of Lionel Hamilton, the Artistic Director of the Royal Theatre, Northampton, and a beautifully evocative description of Jonathan's journey to Cambodia and visiting the monument of Angkor Wat, we come eventually to the meeting with Richard O'Brien and Jim Sharman that led to Jonathan being the first person ever to speak the first words of *The Rocky Horror Show*. Those words would have made an equally good title for this book.

'I would like, if I may, to take you on a strange journey...'

Timothy West
August 2007

Foreword
by
Joy Blakeman
Reader of the original manuscript and Northampton friend

Dear Reader – step warily along the paths of the wanderings of Jonathan Adams in his collage of thoughts concerning his life and times.

Sometimes as surreal as his art works, this book does not purport to be an accurate autobiography – imagine it as having the artistic input indulged in by film-makers when presenting an established book, often covering themselves with the phrase, 'loosely based upon'.

As an artist and actor Jonathan Adams cannot help but rearrange the truth, embroidering, heightening, dramatising and fancifying in characteristically bizarre flights of comic imagination.

Joy Blakeman

'Freud'

Preface

Who are we?
I don't know who I am – I've never known who I am so, whilst reading these memoirs, be advised that, besides being an artist, I am an actor – a breed of whom it is often claimed has no identity of its own.

In my trundling perambulations through life and in my observations of the Passing Parade perhaps I will not only reveal myself to you but also reveal myself to me. Oh fearful thought!

Already the Half has been called. Fifteen minutes. It is nearing 'Curtain Up'. For God's sake don't even breathe the word 'Macbeth' in my hearing.

Five minutes.

Let's hear a resounding rendition of 'Break a Leg' for my debut in 'Jonathan Adams Exposed'.

I'm all yours now – may God have mercy on your souls.

Jonathan Adams

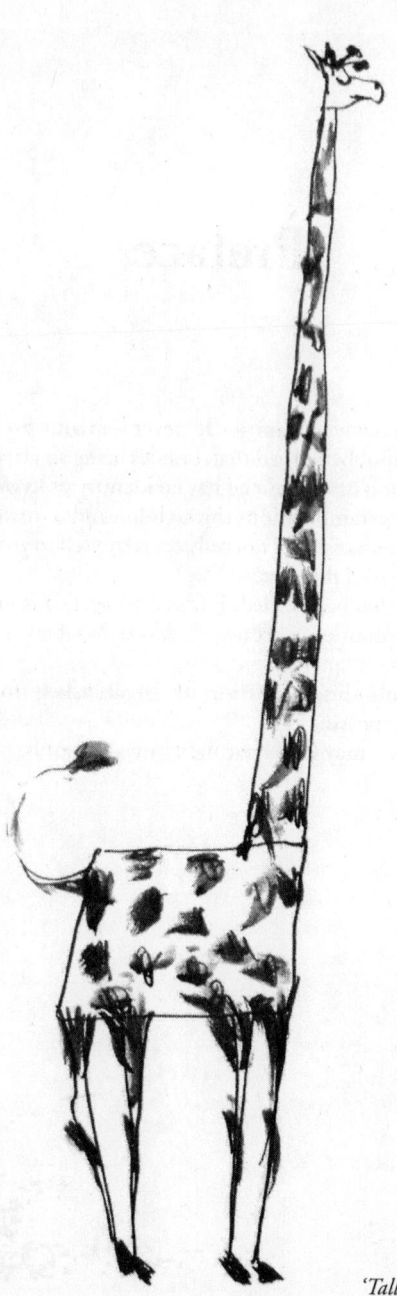

'Tall story'

1
Althorpe

Only a mile or two up the Harlestone Road from St James in Northampton, where I was born, there stands the now doubly famous Althorpe House, a drab and dappled grey pile, brooding four square over a motionless eighteenth-century landscape, and a lake, fashioned in the shape of an ovoid, harbouring a secretive-looking island, now the tomb of a princess. Dense woodland bears down and attempts to enclose the lake.

A seemingly endless wall snakes around the estate, once ruled over by the Red Earl (red only of tonsure.) To the north-east, by the lake, is a temple with a portico of four Roman Doric columns and a pediment.

From the bustle of St James and its dark, urban parks, it was not far for me to pedal on my bicycle to this empty, mysterious domain, before the gossiping crowds came, or to catch a green United Counties bus, which took one much of the way to this Althorpe – or was it Althrup, as the locals are wont to call it – or Althop? or Alfrop? or ... Alf Thrup?

I was told that there was even a tiny railway station with one platform hidden amongst thickening foliage, by the Northampton to Long Buckby railway line, once used by the Red Earl and his lady to meet Royalty and their entourage when it came to stay. I never seemed to be able to find it. In certain favoured positions one could see across the parterre, the majestic stables – built in golden ironstone and, some would say, more beautiful than the 'Big House' itself. They are in the manner of Inigo Jones who designed St James, the Actors' Church in Covent Garden.

Little did I think then that this artificial and mannered landscape would be part of the setting of a Royal drama that rocked the nation and plunged it into a frenzied ferment some half a century later.

'The Curse of Althrop' – A Drama – Time 1998

Dramatis Personae
A princess
A prince

A young earl – entrepreneur and scourge of the Royal Family
A doughty duchess – rude in health (and wealth)
A fairy-tale stepmother – with an aesthetic sense inherited from her mother
Dame BaBaRa – an immensely fluffy, pretty, pink-tinted authoress
A crooning clown – with chords
A long-haired mystic music meister
Dodi – a Lounge Lizard and dodo
Mahamoud Ali Fayed – favourite CD: 'Rule Britannia' played at the Last Night of the Proms
Max Cliff-Hanger – from the Litterati hunting pack
The Paparazzi – hunting pack
The Glitterati – celebs pack
The Marketing Manager – for Flora Margarine
Camilla Parker Bowls – a hunting woman and good egg, according to taste
The Royals – a family stalked by the hideous spectre of MISCEGENATION

Now read on…

I meet the Earl

It was half a century back when I found myself perambulating the grounds of Althorpe with two new friends (Pidcock and Champion). I had just become an art student. We arrived at the mansion by way of the north ha-ha. The sun was beginning to set and long shadows were already unfolding across the landscape and across the darkening facade.

We had been talking about the political situation and the new socialism under the Prime Minister, Mr Atlee. Was it true that the working class were putting coal in the baths of their new houses? Would the Earls of England be shot and their property expropriated? Ah! Bliss would it be in that dawn to be alive! Head bowed in those cruel thoughts, I looked up to see, in the near distance, the very Earl Spencer himself sitting in a wickerwork chair – embroidering.

Fired by our previous political ruminations and suddenly confronted with a living representative of a family that had not long ago functioned as mere proletarian sheep-farmers in Wormleighton, I swung round at a sharp angle of 45 degrees and began to bear down upon the Earl.

Fully intending to deliver him a lecture, or curse him with a red fatwa extolling the expropriation of property, I summoned Pidcock and Champion to follow me, which they did, falteringly.

We stopped, facing the Earl, who raised his head and jumped with a surprised stare, causing his wickerwork seat to creak and his embroidery to fall.

My brain momentarily atrophied and a long time seemed to pass before, blushing in a humble and bourgeois manner, I said, 'Hi! Er – can – er – may we see your pitchers – er – pictures?'

'What, *now*?!' The Earl's visage was bucolic as he picked up his embroidery.

'Well – er – not now that is if you're knitting – er – crochetty – er – crocheting. You see, we are students of the local art school here. You know – St George's Avenue? We are very interested in your pictures. I hear you have some Gainsborough Girls – er – some girls by Gainsborough – from Gainsborough – some girlies…'

'Look, arrange an official visit of your college and we'll go from there. Good afternoon,' and the Earl resumed his work.

'Er, ah, thank you,' I said. 'Come on boys!' And I led the way back…

The sun was casting longer shadows on the parterre and facade as we walked back to the great gates, which were about to close – soon the ha-ha would become invisible, which it had been all along.

I confirmed that the Earl did own some Gainsboroughs. He was one of my favourite old masters.

Weeks later, I happened to join a party of architects who were to be shown round by the Earl. I noticed that he caught my eye and winced. We gathered inside the great entrance hall, said to be the noblest Georgian Hall in the county, heaving with paintings of hunt, hound and horse by J. Wooton.

As we were let in, the Earl was carping about his inability to engage cleaning ladies and skivvies these days and would the ladies take off their stilettos to prevent them further distressing the wooden floors. Luckily there were no ladies with us as architecture was fast gripped by the male domain in those days.

When we were all assembled, we crept, respectfully, into the interior, following the Earl as he detailed another world of deep-coffered coving in the corner; cartouches; curved cornices; cherubs; deeply coved ceilings (MacVicar Anderson, 1877) – '*Don't touch*' – the balustrading of the balcony with dumbbell balusters – 'Don't touch, *please*!' – Houghton, Holkham, Hagley, Vanbrughian details everywhere – Van Aken, Van Somer, Vanderbank, Van der Veld, Van Goyan, Van Mergeren, Van Dick, Van Dyck, Dick Van Dyck, Snyders, Landseer, all in the thick of the hunt tearing the bleeding flesh from deer – '*Don't touch!*' – snarling fangs … stags at bay … the horn blasting… the lurchers growling … tally ho, tally ho, tally ho, *tally hoh*…

Suddenly we were aware of an itinerant workman, obviously a member of the working classes, peering through a window at our group.

The Earl's visage grew rubicund and, striding to the window, gesticulated that he should remove himself forthwith.

I shall never forget the response shouted through the glass, luckily muffled and which I couldn't hear, but decipherable through lip-reading, which I had lately been studying:

'…you fuggin acehole don't you tell me to fuggough mister – you puguglyfugginphoiker – I mean – git off your fat ass and buggeroff…'

Silence.

Paralysis.

'We'll move on,' said the Earl. 'As I was saying – strong turned balusters, the hippy – um – hip-hopped roof pilasters, three bay, pediment, charming frieze again coved circular tapering spiral fluted shafts left and right Lysicrates Monumentali…'

'Yes, he's a very level-headed boy'

2
Family

Dallington

Why I write at length and in such detail and familiarity concerning these dramas is because my grandparents were, symbiotically, linked to the Red Earl of Althorpe. They were the tenant farmers of the estate and lived in the nearby village of Dallington. My mother was in service there for some time. I remember her telling of the Red Earl being annoyed with her for allowing the edge of some underwear to protrude from the corner of an ill-closed drawer.

Surprisingly, this tiny village is still there and hardly changed – almshouses (1673) – a school (1840) – a twelfth-century church in which my baby brother and I were christened – a vicarage (1741) in which lived a vicar and his son James Perry with whom I liked to play on huge lawns covered in crocuses, or indulge in the terrors of hide and seek in the dark, forgotten corners of the vicarage.

Nearby was a 'home' for Barnardo boys. They were to be seen walking in 'crocodiles' for their exercise. We passed them one day and they sneered at us for some reason. James upbraided them saying, 'Don't make faces at us – we give you money.'

In Dallington there was a willow growing aslant a brook that eddied forth through the vicarage garden, purling, from under a little bridge, round the green.

With my jam jar and bandy net, I looked for miller's thumb and spined loach for my aquarium, sticklebacks, crested newts, waterboatmen and frogspawn. You might see the ouzel cock fly by, easily spotted by its black hue and tawny bill.

The water gurgles past the only shop in the village – Minnie Bonham's Emporium for sweets and buttons, where my mother would grumble about Doris Hicks turning the whole shop upside down to purchase a farthing's worth of jelly babies while she waited for service.

Behind the shop was Dallington Hall, a sandy coloured eighteenth-century building in which my mother was to serve as a Red Cross Auxiliary Nurse during the Great War – just a small hop for her from the Althorpe farm and over the road to the hall, which had become a convalescent home for soldiers.

I never knew my maternal grandfather and harbour but one mouldering photograph of him, sepia-tinted, that has almost faded away.

I also harbour a mouldering cutting from the *Northampton Mercury & Herald* newspaper, speaking of his death at seventy-one years of age.

'FREDERICK FARMER: R.I.P.'

'BEGAN FARMING WITH ONLY ONE COW' runs the banner headline. (This would have pleased Lloyd George, and his promised 'One acre and a cow for everyone'.)

'PRIZE WINNER – FAT STOCK SHOWS' screams this Victorian tabloid.

'Member of National Farmers' Union – politically radical' (I wonder what his industrial relations with the Red Earl were like?)

'One of original members – Dallington Parish Council – 29 years overseer – Parish constable'

Only lately have I come to learn that my grandfather was not quite the paragon I seemed to hear of in earlier days. On Saturdays, when the cattle market began to dismantle for the day, Mr Farmer was known to disappear into the ale-house next to the cattle market and the money earned that morning would be squandered in the pursuit of grog and largesse to fellow farmers.

My grandmother had a tough time keeping eight children quiet. They should be seen and not heard in those days.

My grandmother, aged ninety, was dressed in black, silent and immobile, sitting by the hearth. She had long been blind with glaucoma. Her mind was in place and I enjoyed conversation with her – she gave me a novel by Victor Hugo that told of a working man who, against all odds, and by dint of hard work, reached an important position in the world. The ethos of Betterment! She could be quite firm.

In my grandmother's cupboard was a stamp album with an embossed cover containing a collection of very old stamps that were in use in Queen Victoria's time, after 1840, mounted in the conventionally correct spaces delineated for them, which also catered for errant stamps of delinquent size – like the triangular Cape of Good Hope, stamps twice as long as they should be, round stamps, octagonal stamps and oblong stamps. 'Fiscal' stamps or 'Postage Due' were not to be included in any decent collection.

Unfortunately, the stamps were stuck to the page with thick gum – now a dark brown – and anticipating that I might be granted this album one sad day, amidst tears and mourning, foresaw difficulties in removing the stamps from their gummy bed and lamented the prospect of the collection's ruination before it could be transferred to my own album.

On the death of my grandmother, the effects were sold by auction in the garden. The stamp album was nowhere to be seen…

I was fascinated by postage stamps. That made me a philatelist. During times of illness, it would be a real pleasure to be in bed, sweating with scarlet fever, or some such infection popular in those days, or mumps, poring over my 'Simplex' stamp album. The doctor said it should be burned in case it was infectious, but it escaped. My parents didn't insist on it because it would have broken my heart.

The names of the lands these stamps came from were fabulous and unreachable:

Amoy	Moldo-Wallachia
Annam and Tonquin	Thurn and Taxis
Cook Islands	Togo
Dahomey	Van Diemens Land
Djibouti	Zanzibar
Fernando Po	Spice Islands
Foochow	Sandwich Islands
Funchal	Heligoland

Today you can board a Concorde and, within a few hours, be sitting by a man-made shimmering blue pool in one of these exotic destinations while the inhabitants are murdering each other that day down the road.

Some of the countries have disappeared or changed their names. You think that Upper Volta is called Upper Volta? Well, Mr Mastermind! It is called Burkina Faso. I gained a good knowledge of Geography and could summon up all the rulers of the world from Queen Victoria, when you had to lick her back on the Penny Black, to Bolivar, Papa Doc, the Kaiser, King Farouk, Queen Astrid (with the black perforations of death) to the Maharajah of Jhalawar, all knowledge gained from the educational cornucopia of *stamps*.

There was quite a trade in stamps in the playground during tuck-time, and there were what we called 'Approvals' for sale, where you sent away to a dealer, advertising in the *Boys' Own* paper, for a sheet of over-priced stamps, which you then attempted to sell to your mates at 40% profit and return those left.

Today, no children seem to be interested in stamps, probably because nobody writes letters, but are willing martyrs to the computer.

When I pass a shop selling stamps, I always stop and gaze raptly at them. The name 'Stanley Gibbons' is like a mantra to me.

Yes, in other fields I was something of an entrepreneur. I bought a load of very old gramophone records from junk shops – dance bands, crooners, swing, sentimental songs, comic recitations and what you will. I formed a music library of these worn, scratched and generally degenerate discs and charged members 3d per week to hire them out. Hambridge L. of 5 Lower B never returned some of them – the bastard!

Also in my grandmother's cupboard was a musty and pungent-smelling copy of John Bunyan's *Pilgrim's Progress* with tooled black leather cover and gold-edged leaves. It was illustrated with engravings, bespeckled with mildew, of Bunyan's vision – figures, robed or in armour, who had been to Hell and back – Good and Evil, which I looked at with disturbed fascination – Apollyon, The Foul Fiend, the Giant Despair, Mr Lovelust, Faithful burning in Vanity Fair and, eventually, the joy of reaching the Celestial City…

When I was a member of the BBC Radio Drama Repertory Company we spent some days recording the whole of *Pilgrim's Progress* with cuts and lots of coffee…

We were working our way through this humourless phantasmagoria one Sunday when there was a great pause and silence from our producer, Glyn Dearman, as he mulled over the text to sort out some dramatic problem. As we waited to continue, Glyn gave a little giggle.

I enquired, 'Have you found a joke?'

My Auntie Midge looked after Grandma. I think she found it a strain. She was called Midge, for Margaret, but for a Midge she was not midget-sized. She was the youngest but one of the eight children and the only one that remained a spinster. For our family she was quite adventurous, going to Abbeville as a military nurse in the First World War and then living in California for a while. Here, that great repository of cracked religions held sway over her and she became a Jehovah's Witness. In response to their belief that Adam and Eve were originally put on this earth as ready-mades, in pristine condition, I would probe her with the question, 'Did Adam have a belly-button?'

The idiosyncratic nomenclature of 'Midge, the midget' or 'the Mighty Midge' leads us to another unnerving anomaly – that of Auntie Dick.

The name 'Dick', you might suppose, relates more to the masculine gender, but this misnomer merely signifies that, as a child, she behaved like a tomboy.

Dick's name was Alice.

Auntie Dick was the liveliest and most outspoken of the aunties and the most generous. She married Uncle George, a detective inspector. They lived in Barking and, when it was safe to visit London towards the end of the war, my brother (Hi, Pete!) and I sometimes stayed with them.

My Auntie was keen on smartness, making me clean my black, shiny shoes with Cherry Blossom boot polish, comb my hair and even wash it. Not darn socks. That was a woman's job.

Auntie Gert was the oldest member of the Farmer children. In her youth she was in service with the Spencers at Althorpe with my mother. She bore five children but three died. Edie was twenty-one and died of TB. She looked beautiful from the photographs – prettier than most of us Farmer tribe with our large-boned frames and peasant faces, after Breugel.

Three of the family went out to Canada to farm just before the First World War. With the exception of one cousin, who returned for occasional holidays, we never saw them again.

That left Frank who was, for a time, the publican of the Brington pub, a mile or two from Althorpe, and who then went on to manage a smallholding with my Auntie Annie. They had some evil-looking vicious white ferrets that snarled and shook their cages. I hate to see caged animals and birds.

The youngest child was our mother, Louisa. She was to die much sooner than the others, at the age of forty-nine, and beat her brothers and sisters to the Endgame. My brother was then eleven. I was sixteen.

'Orbiston'

When I was five my mother took me to the school just around the corner, called 'Orbiston' – a dames' academy for girls but laced with a few little boys as was the fashion then. This stopped them having to engage in the rough and tumble of the nearby elementary school; it was deemed unwise for the two groups to meet socially.

My mother delivered me to the gate and, as she left, I cried. I was put to the 'sand pit' and this calmed me down.

We Orbistonians were quite decorative in our smart purple jackets and caps as we wove our way up Harlestone Road and then, in a line, along the enclosing walls of Dallington Park on a nature walk. We had to be particularly well-behaved when we saw the Misses Butcher approaching.

These ladies were the one-time headteachers and owners of Orbiston before a Miss Rolls took over as headmistress. They seemed to be omnipresent, suddenly materialising round the corner with a faint, knowing smile, by the park-keeper's bright green shed or the dowdy pavilion with its kids' scribblings on the walls – 'I love Brenda'.

The school was really a gaunt Victorian terraced house pretending to be a school, comprising one gloomy room and kitchen below with a wireless in the corner for the transmission of the King's speeches and the messages of Mr Chamberlain, should they approach the microphone, and one large room above, which could be made into two classrooms by the use of sliding doors. These were trundled apart for hymns and prayers and we sat on the rough wooden floor facing the teacher on her dais. I was exquisitely sensitive to the tactile quality of this flooring, constantly suffering splinters in my bottom owing to restlessness, which resulted in my being frequently propelled down to the lavatory by a prefect to have the pointed chips extracted.

Behind the house was a garden cum diminutive sports' area with a lawn and a grass bank to roll down. On sports days we would perform the three-legged race, the sack race, the egg and spoon race, netball and rounders, so I am fully conversant with games for the female sex.

A Miss Oakey taught the pianoforte and I had lessons in her dark house opposite the school. The walls were adorned with grey prints of Beethoven, Brahms and Bach, and a statue of the head of Wagner, the colour of pale custard. I studied, at my request, pieces from 'Snow White and the Seven Dwarfs' and she told my mother that I had a strong rhythmic sense, though boogie-woogie had not yet reached these parts. It was deemed good that I should learn to play the piano.

Academically I floated through the sewing and the times tables and sums. I used to wander back home in the middle of the morning thinking it was dinner time and a prefect would be sent to the house to retrieve me.

The headmistress told my mother, 'School rules never apply to John.'

Altogether, I had a pleasant time in my five years at Orbiston and made one or two special friends. John Chaplin, my chum, son of the vicar of the most deprived part of Northampton, lived next to the LMS goods yards, which shunted all through the night, but, upon entering the undulating vicarage garden, it was discovered to be enormous, containing, as it did, the rudimentary ruins of Northampton Castle, covered in ivy and all but disappeared.

There remains a tiny door, which opens on to roaring traffic. A dramatic place to weave spells in. I wondered if the ghost of King John had fled when the railway came to Northampton.

James Perry, yet another vicar's son from Dallington, was a boy of haughty mien, and I remember John Champion, a nervous orange-haired boy about whom we will hear later (if there is room on these pages).

But my special, special friend was an older girl called Mimi, from Austria. I suppose she was a refugee from the Nazis. I was in love with her – she was voluptuous (I didn't know that word then, but with behindsight, that's what she was) and of a gay disposition. (I am attempting here to reinstate this word to its original meaning). She was different from the other girls.

I said, 'I'm going to marry Mimi.'

I went to an Orbiston Old Girls' reunion some years ago and met Miss Rolls again, then in her eighties. The women at the celebration were surprised and suspicious seeing an elderly man joining them and declaring himself to be just 'an old boy passing through…'.

'I remember you,' said Miss Rolls. 'You lived just round the corner. You were going to marry Mimi.'

Mother

In my very young days, mother was a strongly built but nervous woman who would jump at slight noises and say, 'Hark!' These responses became more frequent when the war broke out.

She was excitable and so garrulous that, in my younger days, I would tug at her hand, grousing, 'Oh, come on, Mum, I'm tired!' or use any such other good reason for the termination of ladies' chatter.

Callers at the front door would make her apprehensive. We lived near to one of the town's mental asylums, 'Berry Wood'. Its monumental Victorian clock tower dominated the surrounding countryside and the inexorably creeping suburbia. The inmates incarcerated here were from the poorer classes, sometimes put there for the whole of their lives. Some were committed on a pretext.

I saw many of these people's heads, which were just visible above the tall, dark red wall, as they ambled backwards and forwards, caged in beautiful gardens. The walled area I was privy to contained elderly men, though I could only see their cloth caps. The head of a bright white-starched nurse talking to an inmate might occasionally also be seen.

Some of these ruined people were allowed to wander out into the world in their bemused or angry state and called repeatedly at No 89. You could see a blurred image through the frosted glass of our front door. The dark stranger had rung the bell and wanted to give my mother a 'message from the unknown'.

My frightened mother would say, whilst politely shutting the door, 'Excuse me, I'll fetch my husband.'

My father would be at the factory, so she would run to the back yard and call over the wall to Mrs Lewis to see if her husband was in. Looking down the hall corridor, one would see the sinister silhouette still lurking there, stationary, waiting…

With good fortune, Mr Lewis would come out into 'The Backs' and frighten off the man with mention of the police. If Mr and Mrs Lewis were not in, we just locked ourselves in and waited until the figure dematerialised. We had no telephone.

In lighter, picturesque vein, French onion-sellers were a particular bête noire of mother. She told us that once, in a fit of pique, she refused an offer of onions. As this seller walked away, leaving the front gate open, she called after him, 'Fermez la porte!'

His riposte was, 'Shut it y'self, missus, avec knobs on!'

My mother had rather conventional attitudes – she didn't like to see washing hanging on the line on a Sunday and was particularly critical of others when the Bishop visited Dallington during a church celebration and observed the windy flapping of long johns and Marks & Spencer's underpants. It was apposite that the hit of the day would soon be 'We're Going To Hang Out The Washing On The Siegfried Line'.

It was at this Diocesan event in the village that the saga of the sugar was enacted, and where I felt embarrassed for my mother. The people attending the open-air service had trickled into the parish room and had settled down for a rustic beano around a long, large trestle table, draped in white, neat, embroidered cloths. Helpers were bringing round sandwiches and cups of tea. My mother was responsible for filling the sugar bowls. Soon the party was tucking in and tea was being served. Within a few minutes we sensed a corrosion of this happy atmosphere of well-being. A sudden explosion of retching and vomiting and gastroperturbationandregurgitation ensued.

An old village soul shouted out, 'It's the sugar doin' it!'

My mother said, 'What's the matter with the sugar?'

The old soul shouted, 'Sugar!? It's salt, me duck!'

My mother, blushing wildly, disappeared into the kitchen. The Bishop sat back safe and sound, as he was not an imbiber of tea, and tried to defuse the situation by philosophising on the story of Lot's wife…

How I met Dennis the Dachshund

The children of the forties and fifties (probably mainly those from middle-class homes) were the devoted tiny slaves of teatime radio. I used to squat on a humpty, ear close to the speaker, avidly listening to the daily 'Children's Hour' presented by the gentlemenly Uncle Mac and Uncle David. I always enjoyed 'Toy Town'. Even to this day, I will give superb imitations of the characters – the Mayor, Mr Grouser, the Inventor, Larry the Lamb, Ernest the Policeman – to anybody, in fact, who will listen (now, mostly, quite old people). 'Children's Hour' was taken off the air in the early fifties. Children throughout the land cried. 'Toy Town' was dead.

My favourite character was Dennis the Dachshund, friend of Larry the Lamb, who spoke a tortured, convoluted kraut lingua. (Racist? Never mind, they started the war.)

When I became an actor I needed a dialect coach and was recommended to a certain Mr Jack, a BBC radio actor and Boy Scout leader of the Finchley troop. Apparently he could spot the variations in dialect between each city in every country. He was also an authority on the whole spectrum of canine sounds: when I asked Mr Jack for a Dusseldorf accent, he asked, 'Which street in Dusseldorf?'

'Toy Town' was written by a certain S. G. Hulme Beaman. You could purchase little two-dimensional wooden fretwork models of Toy Town figures and also illustrated books.

I was 'tickled pink' to learn that I was being coached by a one-time German sausage-dog – something more than a hound dog, I think.

I had the pleasure of meeting Uncle David (Mr Mayor) in later years at a radio party where he, then an octogenarian, rued the fact that radio work no longer came his way, despite his desire to continue broadcasting.

The Passing Parade

The front room of No 89, sometimes known as the drawing-room, was cold and inhospitable when I was growing up. It was never used, but was preserved ready for the guests that never came. The best silver cutlery, Sheffield-made, wrapped in tissue paper, was ready in a drawer with serviettes of pristine white linen, virgin to this day. On the empty mantleshelf stood a very heavy, old, black marble clock. Every evening my father or mother would complete a ritual of winding up the clock. 'Have you done it tonight, Dad?'

A smell of new but slightly dusty fabric permeated the sofa, armchairs and overstuffed, plumped-up cushions. The heavy grey curtains were rarely drawn except in a heat wave or when it was known that a funeral would be passing by. In those days it was customary for gentlemen in the street to doff their hats as a mark of respect to the dead. When I went to my mother's funeral and saw people observing this ritual, I was touched.

The pictures on the walls of our house were by a man called Mr Morley, of no pretension, who specialised in painting scenes of bored sheep driven home in the sunset by a very old, drunken shepherd, or sailing ships in a Turneresque mist – 'pot-boilers' he would call them, and my father 'studied' art with him in the early days, attempting to master the Morley watercolour technique.

A bookcase contained some yachting magazines (the food of dreams), gardening books (the food of the flowers) and *Escape from the Soviets*.

The piano bore the legend 'Laurent'. I touched it only when I had to do piano practice for Miss Oakey.

There was no aspidistra in our window, as there was in most of the houses down the road. We were a cut above that.

I sometimes positioned myself on a pouffe in the bay window and observed the Passing Parade. The window became my picture frame – a screen depicting suburban dramas. Before me, the mise en scène: hedging, bushes, hawthorn and the rough hillocks over the other side of the road where we played, behind which were allotments. To the left, far back, a new elementary school was being erected in which I was later to teach.

To the right a 'Tudor' vicarage was surrounded by enormous elms that swayed as the winter wind whined, raucous with cawing rooks.

The Vicar's daughter, Catherine, was nice to play with. It seemed that God now arranged for me the friendship of children whose parents were of the cloth.

The melancholy of a Sunday afternoon

The melancholy of a Sunday afternoon was perpetuated by people parading in their Sunday best, holding sprays of daffodils on their way to the cemetery where my grandma is buried.

Easter Sunday morn: 'Hot cross buns – hot cross buns – hot cross buns – hot cross buns…,' calls the boy with a baker's wicker basket full of them.

'Stop me and buy one,' reads the ice-cream man on wheels.

Sunday November 11th, eleven am… Everyone suddenly stops … silence … men take off their trilby hats. A minute. It is not long before the stillness is released … a distant bugle from the Doddridge Chapel … life cranks up once more.

Ah! Here come the elephants, ambling very slowly with their trunks and tails intertwined, accompanied by a savage youth wielding a stick. These pachyderms will be lumbering past the cemetery to their quarters up the road at Hopping Hill. They perform in Chipperfields circus.

If my father learned that they were coming up the road it was All Systems Go – this was becoming a race with one of the neighbours! My father would grab a bucket and shovel and stand by. When an elephantine dollop was dropped, he was out there with me, like greased Sabu the Elephant Boy. Our garden developed an extraordinary degree of fertility. I swore that the vegetables next door looked weedier than ours.

A poet, beautiful and biblical-like, with the statutory long hair, beard and sandals, padded up the road for a walk with his young wife and child. Keats must have looked like this. He was a Conchie (a breed much hated by my father). He wrote a novel *From This Foundation*, which was set in St James and featured the local characters (in disguise). The locals found out and were very angry with this portrait of themselves 'scribbled by a tight-arsed interlexual. What a bloody cheek me duck!' I have been hunting down this book for decades without success.

When I was in my teens the poet and his wife were kind and helpful to me, encouraging me in my 'creative work' and accepting my gauche manners. I told them I didn't believe in manners, but le bête sauvage. My father told them I'd grow out of it.

The poet was a translator of Japanese poetry, by the way, and went off with an actress from the Repertory Theatre and a few haiku.

Once I saw a tableau in the window of the painting and decorating shop that I still cannot understand but have to accept as a mystery: a little girl, quite naked, stood slowly turning the pages of a wallpaper sample book placed on a stand. She appeared to be existing in her own world and oblivious to any passer-by. The few who did pass by and caught a glimpse of this scene hurried on, pretending not to notice.

The Avenue

A world away from the mean red-brick houses that comprised the main body of St James (Jimmy's End), the dwelling places of the workers who cobbled shoes in the monolithic factory of Lewis's, is a crescent called 'The Avenue' –

just off the Harlestone Road – a crescent of Victorian Mansions, designed in many fanciful styles, dark with old trees, heavy with rooks, approached by a rough road 'not adopted' where the rich lived in seclusion. The Barnardo boys lived there as well. It was here that George Lewis, the owner of the shoe factory, lived with his family, for whom my father worked as head clerk for forty years. Lewis and his relations were staunch Congregationalists and this branch of Nonconformism upheld a strong presence in the town. Their saint was Philip Doddridge, a nineteenth-century preacher.

At twelve o'clock on a Sunday morning one could hear the sound of drums and brass bugles: here was Mr George Lewis heading a little army of boys marching in black uniforms with a drum major twirling his baton up the road from Bottom Doddridge Chapel hall to Harlestone Road. This was another quasi army of God, the Boys' Brigade. The drums were stirring. I would run out to listen to them.

Bullying

I have hardly ever been bullied. I avoided confrontation by playing the fool. Compared with children today, I have experienced no deadly encounters with Child Aliens of the third, or any other, kind. Now, because of my advanced age, I am more in tune with the seminal and archetypal figures of yesteryear: Mickey Mouse and Desperate Dan. The vulnerability of flesh and blood has only intruded painfully on a few occasions. Take, for instance, fishing near Dallington village with my next door dear pal (or so I thought him to be) – Roger.

A much older boy approached us, seized my jam jar containing sticklebacks, threw it to the ground and unctuously told us we were trespassing. My pal could only giggle. We retreated. I was frightened and angry but powerless.

Another time, out in 'The Backs', I was seized by two older boys who, having lured me into their garage, pounced on me and began tying me to a chair. When I began to cry one of the boys, who obviously felt guilty, urged, 'OK. Leave him be.' I stumbled off and broke into a run. Had they previously been watching a gangster film? My father called at their home and the mother berated the sons, who stood by sheepishly.

My father could wield a hefty slap and, if he approached me to deliver one, my protective mother would flush and call me inside. When I accidentally damaged something, he would refer to this accident as 'Sabotage' or berate me for my paucity of intelligence.

One incident, though, gives me food for thought whilst I toss and turn on my bed of pain, wondering if I am the man I ought to be, or would have been if what had happened hadn't happened.

Roger, the boy next door, who suffered from a heavy duty excess of eczema, used to play with me and my baby brother in the garden. Suddenly, this boy, for no cogent reason, delivered me an almighty crack across the skull with a cricket bat. While he giggled I fainted from the attack. As the minutes ticked by, a protuberance on my forehead grew to enormous proportions.

I just wonder if my apparent lifelong languor and wilting concentration has its origins in that skull-thumping crack on the frontal lobes. I think I may be, unknowingly, a neuropathologicalmunchausen sufferer by proxy.

Roger loved a good, supportive giggle; I observed him from an upstairs window in the yard as he watched his father screwing a cockerel's neck, after which it flapped around headless in circles, spurting blood. His giggles echoed in the back yard.

My brother was also a victim on one occasion when my father, for some unaccountable reason, had moved a railway sleeper into our garden. My devilish pal was levering it about so dangerously that my innocent brother sustained a painful injury to his foot. The 'pal' found this amusing and howled with peals of laughter.

Now that I look back, there seemed to be mysterious accidents at times that sorely tested the Law of Averages.

Who am I to plead for the understanding of my fellow boys? I was not totally blameless. To my shame I remember filling my air gun with earth and walking up to where my father was talking to an elderly neighbour. Unprovoked, I proceeded to shoot her in the face, splattering her with earth. Mrs Chipperfield reeled back (luckily she wore glasses) and my father seized the gun and broke it over his thigh, sending me indoors. I have absolutely no idea why I did this. Perhaps Roger was equally mystified by his lethal dexterity with a cricket bat.

In bed in the depth of the night, I wonder where that kid from Gehenna is. Sometimes I wake up sweating, thinking I hear that eldritch giggling again from so long ago.

Bexhill

In 1939 war was brooding and the family went 'down to the seaside' for what proved to be the last time – Bexhill-on-Sea. At last, the August Bank Holiday week had arrived when the shoe factories emptied their leathery maws and let loose their workers for a week of fun by the seaside, if they could afford it.

The delivery horse and cart from the LMS railway station in Northampton had taken away our trunk, which my father, a man of infinite patience, had spent a whole night packing with miraculous precision and an almost scientific sense of cubic capacity and space. My cousin Harold took us in his taxi to the station where we would catch the train and later retrieve the luggage in the hotel.

As was our custom, we arrived on the platform just as our train was about to leave. My father grabbed at the carriage door handle, whilst my mother, panting, stumbled behind with us children. An official ran up and slapped him on the wrist shouting, 'Desist!', and the train chugged away.

The atmosphere was 'distressed' for a time. My father was always pathologically late. We sank back into acceptance. We had to wait for a couple of hours – occasionally consuming a 'Five Boys' chocolate bar from a vending machine. 'And don't make yourself sick, John. That's enough!'

Eventually: change at Blisworth, change at Euston for Victoria, change to green electric SR, to Toy Town by the Sea – Bexhill – move into small hotel (baggage already arrived), meet the proprietor's wife and chambermaid who show us to our rooms. The not unpleasant odour of guests and cooking: clean. Water in glasses, glistening. A booming gong to call us to meals. But I was yearning to see my first glimpse of the sea, which was always magical.

There were so many emporia bulging with goodies that you couldn't see the shop frontages. Merchandise hung, cluttered and bursting, with spades, buckets, nets, windmills on sticks, pink sticks of sweet rock enclosing paper pictures of the Bexhill Esplanade. Dad would try and haggle to knock the price down. On a hot, windy day, ochre sand might be blown into ridges on the pink pavement, swirling like a desert around the donkeys' hooves.

Most stalls had a selection of garish postcards with pictures of women of enormous proportions and men who appeared emaciated and brow-beaten.

'Mum, why are these gentlemen so skinny looking?' I asked.

'Never you mind,' she replied.

There was a caption on each postcard at which people used to laugh uproariously. I never understood why. Anyway, mother would pull me away as she would if someone were swearing within earshot.

The newly built de la Warr pavilion was a hymn to ultra-modern functionalism, a light and airy construction of bending, undulating glass and metal. I was fascinated by its presence – it looked like a great liner beached on the sand – it looked outwards to the future, to the sea, air and freedom – not inwards like dark, Victorian halls. I had never seen a building like it. I went to a lecture, in its big hall, on Creatures of the Sea. A professor projected slides through an epidiascope and irritably tapped a cane to signal the next picture as he talked, showing photographs and diagrams of sea monsters with repulsive tentacles. In particular I was disturbed by the Globe Fish.

As we walked along the esplanade I noticed a white-collared, elderly cleric walking very slowly with a boy whom I would later learn was his son. It reminded me of my ecclesiastic pals back home. It so happened that the vicar and son were staying at our hotel and they were seated next to us at meal times.

There was a dark side – I was beginning to be aware of the anxiety that gnaws beneath the sometime bright and jolly Parade of Existence. My father hinted that the vicar was 'ogling' the younger women at a nearby table. I didn't know what this funny-sounding word meant. My mother was critical and taut. There was an 'atmosphere' at the table which I sensed but didn't understand. I felt dread.

This errant holy minister's son, called in those days a 'cripple', moved around with the aid of a crutch, one leg being in 'irons'. One day, after lunch, when everybody seemed to have disappeared, I was standing in the hall when the boy approached me. After talking he suddenly seized me and tried to drag me upstairs. I fought loose, shaking with surprise; the crutch clattered to the floor and I ran to my bedroom. Did I cry? I forget. I didn't tell my parents. (On further reflection it may have been a 'cry for love', as we call it these days.) I kept silent and tried to believe it never happened. I would avoid the boy. My father thought I looked uneasy. Anxiety troubled me.

In the over-warm hotel lounge as evening fell, before being sent to bed with my cup of Horlicks and two biscuits, a 'flapper' would emerge from her room – a voluptuous platinum blonde who was incredibly brown. Over a pre-prandial Pimms No 1 (as she called it) she would exhibit to the guests the sun-kissed and tanned parts of her curvaceous body (that is those parts allowable by law to see the light of day in 1939) to the sound of:

'Cooooo!'

'Wooooo!'

'Gosh!'

'Aren't you *brown*!'

'Aren't-chew-*brow*nnn!'

'You ain' arf br*ow*n!'

'Ow! Look at that!'

Deprecating the seductive charms of her fleshy bloom, she would bring out a cigarette case of Abdullas, with a feline smile, igniting a gold lighter which she flicked open, flashing glossy pink fingernails. It was the first time I had seen a *woman in trousers*, which was still not de rigueur, even in Bexhill.

I noticed that she had what I thought to be a strange way of speaking. I whispered to my father, who, somewhat shy himself, didn't usually attend these little impromptu soirées before the gong and dinner, why was she speaking in this 'funny way'?

My father asked her, politely, where she came from – surely not England?

'Germany!' she replied quickly with an even broader smile than usual.

'Ah!' said my father. 'I have been there! Forgive me saying, Madam, I was there in 14-18 only, what? Twenty or more years ago.'

'Oh! As a soldier?'

'Yes. As a prisoner.'

I dreaded the conversation to come. I knew that Dad could 'go on' about the war if you let him. He rather enjoyed talking about his three and a half years of incarceration in a Munster prison camp, during which he pursued activities like performing music-hall songs, sketching and painting, acting and editorship of the camp magazine. Ironically this was the most creative time of his life – I have three hundred photographs of life in the camp, which was assiduously recorded through the eye of a camera.

'Ha! It's all over now, sir, we're all friends,' broke in the German lady with that flashing smile. Somehow she reminded me of Mimi of Orbiston.

'In any case I was much too young for the war. I was in the kindergarten. As they say, it's all over bar the shouting!' she laughed.

'Oh, I don't know so much,' retorted my father. 'Things are a bit unsettled at the moment.'

'Never, sir. Nothing will happen. Germany and Great Britain – we are friends you know. Ja! I come from, how d'you say it? I come from "upstairs", you know? I am a "Von" Schmidt-Rottluf. Many English people come to our country a lot now, and enjoy our well – strength, eh? Many aristocracy come. They love our, what you say, exciting carnivals by torchlight and all those smart uniforms. I am proud! Sometimes I think we go too far. After all, if people don't like us they can go, but we're a healthy people now – health and efficiency – or rather, efficiency and health – ha? Healthy people now – that's where I get my tan!' and she laughed.

The cleric and his crippled son were hunched in a dark corner of the lounge. The vicar was half asleep but his son was listening, scowling. I felt him looking at me on occasion. I avoided his angry gaze.

'Near my house we have a wonderful solarium which I often go to. Only clean people are allowed in. Pooh!' The guests in the lounge stirred, mildly interested. I was soon sent to bed.

Later…

The German lady was 'caught by the sun' and was no more to be seen.

My father said that they wanted to ask her some questions…

'Who are *they*, Dad?'

I have few memories of my mother on this last holiday: I think it was the beginning of that long fading deterioration that gradually afflicted her and she was starting to drift away into her own sad world. She might giggle a little, or complain about her eyes.

The atmosphere was clouding over…

3
War

'**P**udowt that light! Doncha know there's a waron?!'

My baby brother hadn't put his light off. It wasn't me! I sat on a humpty, crouching next to the speaker of the radiogram at five minutes to eleven listening to the Home Service on September 3rd 1939. Some minutes past eleven Mr Chamberlain had addressed us and we were at war. All to do with a piece of paper, apparently.

The military infrastructure of the state, already primed by the 'phoney war', was still ill-prepared, although gas masks had already been distributed and it was compulsory to carry these rubber voodoo fetish heads in boxes, over the shoulder, at all times. Gas had been used in the Spanish Civil War, it was said, and Musso had gassed the Abyssinians. As soon as I heard the first siren I put on my mask, anticipating trouble.

'UP UP UP – 144 DOWN' sang the headlines. The country galvanized itself. It was quickly covered with sandbags.

Children were torn from their parents and evacuated from London to places like Northampton. My mother tells how a policeman came round asking if our household would take evacuees. Mother said no, for various reasons. The policeman looked in the window and saw 'plenty of room there, madam.' We were a family of four.

Down the road some evacuees were housed. We used to play with them out in 'The Backs'. Londoners were a bit 'rough' – the East End, you know... In fact, we in Harlestone Road were rougher than them in some respects. The coming of evacuees worked well for the lazy indigenous child, for our grammar school was double-booked, so we worked only in the mornings. Willesden Grammar School, an ugly-looking mob, took it over in the afternoon.

We were called out by Miss Holding, one of our teachers, to pick stinging nettles for the war effort – I'm not sure what they were for, but they could pack a hefty sting if approached rashly, as my father found when he jumped into a bed of them. Why? He was on Home Guard duty in Harlestone Road that night and just missed the delivery of Northampton's bombs.

Back home we heard the deafening bang and Mum grasped my little baby brother and me, pulled us from our beds and made for the cubbyhole under the stairs, which was considered to be the safest place. One bungalow was destroyed but no one killed.

There were three bombs dropped on Northampton, all told. One, aimed at my father, missed, the second demolished part of the St Andrew's lunatic asylum and the third buried itself in the corner of a forgotten field.

'It's all right, it's one of ours!'

A crippled Stirling bomber, from which the crew had baled out, found itself unalterably making its way towards Northampton and the helpless pilot took to his parachute, which failed to open. He was killed. The Stirling hit the main shopping area, ground its way up the street on its belly, wings breaking off, and came to rest in Northampton centre, just missing All Saints Church, its bombs intact. The aircraft had found itself fitting into the small remaining space with no civilian deaths or much damage to buildings.

These monsters of the air could be 'spotted', like trains. I took *The Spotter*, a magazine that included black silhouettes of the latest engine of death. Sitting at table for lunch/dinner (what do you call it?), if we heard a very low, loud British one coming, my baby brother and I would rush out and 'spot' it, whilst mother vainly called us to come back in because the Yorkshire pudding was getting cold. We knew which side the plane was on because of the distinctive sound of the engines.

By now we were hoarding food to support a long-drawn-out war of attrition. We packed the area under the stairs with tins of food and the general necessities of existence.

The keening sirens – with their chilling wail (a sound that still haunts me) – made me blasé and I would go out at night into the backyard and listen to aircraft up in the high blackness – the throbbing engines of the Germans, the measured hum for 'our boys'.

I watched the burning of Coventry from my bedroom window some twenty miles away. 'They're gettin a packit tonight, me duck, and no mistake…'

Mother was now an ARP lady, patrolling the Harlestone Road. It was not good for her increasingly nervous state. She also joined a First Aid team as she had gained experience from her nursing days in Dallington Hall.

We would see more and more American troops take over the town. They were not welcomed by the older generation, or the youth, who feared their potency. It's true, we did say, 'Got any gumchum?' as we worked our way down a convoy of lorries resting along Harlestone Road, like a gang of scruffy beggars.

I looked out from the front room window at the Passing Parade. This time it wasn't elephants that we sometimes saw lumbering up the Harlestone Road, it was the chain-mailed tanks and giant guns. Where had all the elephants gone? Had they been mixed with Spam and eaten in the Civic Restaurants?

Towards the end of the war mother was admitted into hospital on occasion and began losing her earlier brightness. After school I would walk up to the town's General Hospital to visit her. Firstly I saw her in the noisy general ward – 'Spencer'. A sad, rather good-looking, older woman lay opposite her, murmuring continuously, 'Oh dear, oh dear, oh dear, oh dear.' As depressing a companion as one could imagine.

Eventually mother was put into a private, more 'select' ward. Mr Shaw, my mother's specialist, then seemed to take more interest and had time to acknowledge me with a cheerful greeting. Our afternoon meetings, after school, were warm and my mother seemed more relaxed than usual.

Now it was safer to visit my Uncle George and Auntie Dick: the bombing had eased off.

Uncle George was a solid, well-built man. Much of his time was spent on duty in West Ham Stadium and, besides the dogs, he used to take my baby brother and me to watch speedway racing, which I enjoyed with its stink of petrol and the rasping and snarling of the bikes. A version of the sport we transferred back to the Northampton 'Backs' by charging round the blocks on our bikes, just missing the air raid shelter's blind corners and scarcely avoiding civilians – extremely dangerous, and various parents stopped it. My baby brother, Peter, still dreams of those vibrant days and the smell of Speedway, so he tells me.

My florid Uncle George took us about London – round Scotland Yard, the Whispering Gallery of St Paul's, Limehouse, where I saw 'sinister yellow Chinamen' sitting in their vests and shorts on the doorsteps of their slum houses; the endless, eyeless, blank serpentine walls of the docks; Petticoat Lane, where ('twas said) they would lift something from you at one end and you'd find it on offer at the other ... 'Cor blimey, guv' ... 'Lovaduck'...; the oppressive, sooty blackness of the mighty buildings of state, the Admiralty, St Martin's-in-the-Field, the Bank, Gamages (where one could buy anything from a pin to an elephant). St Paul's, still standing, almost unscarred, after the great Blitz night that levelled everything around it because the nation had prayed to God, en masse, for its survival – and it worked. God answered in the affirmative. After all, it was His temple – He'd be cutting off His holy nose to spite His holy visage.

It was on these car rides around London that my flushed Uncle would tell me about the working classes keeping nutty slack in their new baths and how they were queueing up in their thousands to obtain free false teeth that they didn't need; how he saw a photo in the *News of the World* of the new Minister of Education, a Mr Tomlinson, who, when talking to the King, *kept his bowler hat on* – the thundering pig – bloody communism.

My rubefacient Uncle George was no defender of the wet and weak and thought that I, a quiet, gentle soul, was a bit soppy – a privileged pupil in a private hoity-toity *girls'* school, for goodness sake!

I was with my rubescent Uncle George, having tea in the garden of a fellow detective who was giving boxing lessons to his young, loutish son, when my burly Uncle started playfully lunging into me. He seized me and started throwing me about, then round and round, eventually putting me down with a thump.

'Whoops! John. Phew! You've grown heavy,' said my puce Nunkle. 'What d'you want to be when you leave school? A boxer?'

I said, 'An actor.'

My rubicund Uncle roared with laughter.

'An actor! Bless me, you? You couldn't act the skin off a pork sausage, matey. Here you are, you go to this school round the corner – what's it called? – OrrBiston! – Orbissturm! – Or*biston*! – you'll end up a pansy! Ha, ha, sonny boy – you're too *quiet* to be an actor.'

'Yes, Uncle,' I said.

'Do you like boxing, John?'

'Not really, Uncle.'

'Have a go, Joe! Come on – put on the gloves and Jimmy here will show you the ropes. Don't hurt him, Jim.'

Jim sneered, 'Put on the gloves and go, go, go, Mr Or*biston*, GO!!!'

At that moment I hated my flatulent Uncle George, with his playful but demeaning bullying, and with whom I was ill at ease. I could feel a blush rising on my cheeks at the possibility of 'looking silly' in front of my plethoric Uncle George and the other detective and his cocksure son. I also feared getting hurt.

We put on the gloves and, before I could say Joe Louis, the lout came in towards me and started teasing me with feather-like punches that seemed to get harder and harder. Taken aback, an irritation and fear began to rise in me and I went to hit back. This seemed to release a dormant power in me and I returned fire, increasing my punches in a style that seemed to come naturally. Emboldened by an aggressive fluency I had begun to upset the lout.

At this point his father moved forward and stopped the bout with a 'That'll do, son.'

My Brylcremed Uncle George was taken aback by my instinctive display of boxing skill.

When we got home he obviously saw me in a new light.

'Well done, son,' my beefed-up Uncle said. 'I didn't know you had it in you.'

I must confess that I felt chuffed (as the saying goes).

One neighbour had a daughter Brenda, of my age, fifteen, and we met sometimes. We were packed off to *Iolanthe* in the West End Theatre and Arthur Askey and the Crazy Gang at the Victoria Palace.

The daughter was sad; her stepmother was a wicked stepmother from the school of Grimm and didn't like Brenda, behaving jealously towards her, but the father was a likeable man.

Later, Brenda and I used to linger together in the bomb shelter in my sanguine Uncle and Aunt's garden to indulge in talk and playing games. I once caught sight of her delightfully downy armpits. Perhaps sensing this attraction she demonstrated a little custom the girls had in her school. She recited to me an erotic mantra:

'A kiss. A cuddle? A…!'

Here, the teller would demonstrate the sexual act by positioning the pointed forefinger of one hand through an aperture made by the thumb and forefinger of the other hand. This was as far as the said mimic presentation went. Easy really.

My rubiginous Uncle George was not laggardly in picking up any sex radar or inventing 'goings on' in the shelter – the Grande Palais de Venus – with a bit of joshing.

'Oy-yoi-yoi! You all right, you two???'

The naughty naughtiness embarrassed me.

Forays to the shelter continued and the ambience was, as ever, genteel. I didn't rock the boat.

'Criminal'

4
School days

*'School days, school days,
Oh! Those golden rule days'*

After Orbiston I arrived at my second school, Northampton Grammar School for Boys, which was less cosy than my previous school, probably because there were no little girls present, but brutal boys.

I was with my 'pal' John Chaplin and we found ourselves in Form One Lower, which studied in a mock-Tudor house opposite the main school.

On the first day, the teacher, a Miss Holding, went through the register checking names and details; it was found that I was in the wrong class, so I was taken by Miss Holding to another class – Form One Upper – which was in the forbidding main building. Here Miss Holding delivered me to the form master, the Art Teacher, Mr Baxter, a skeletal man with a skin like shiny yellow parchment and an enigmatic sense of humour. I was allocated a place and Miss Holding left.

It wasn't long before she returned bringing my pal, John Chaplin, into the room, crying. He wanted to be with me.

And so it was granted.

In Form One Upper, Mr (Bertie) Baxter was extremely popular, as his art lessons consisted mainly of his telling adventure stories – gangsters in Chicago ('I saw a chicken cross West 44th Street') and tales of Ali Baba. Our paintings were illustrations of these Arabic tales plus some exercises in pattern-making and colour-mixing and, of course, a white cube, cone, cylinder, or a deckchair for older pupils to copy. Mr Baxter's pièce de résistance was his picture of a Spitfire attacking Jerry – we would crowd round his desk as he brought it out to give it an airing and even perhaps pin it up for a bit. We gazed with wonder at his brilliant watercolour technique – the sheen of Spitfire metal and the shine of the Messerschmitt's transparent gun turrets.

Mr Baxter's wife was French – she taught the odd day at school and we boys used to vie with each other in springing up to open the door for her when she wished to enter the masters' common room. A thick grey miasma of tobacco smoke would be revealed hanging round the teachers.

Mr Bascomb was the other member of the Lower and Upper School triumvirate – an imposing figure with wobbling, fleshy blue, pouchy jowls and lips, and very professorial gold pince-nez. He was on the board of the Repertory Theatre and his brother was an actor there, a thespian loose of spittle and thus a danger to the front row.

One day we had settled down when a boy entered who had been summoned – for bullying. Mr Bascomb asked if what he had heard was true and the boy muttered something. He was dealt such a blow on the head that the boy keeled over, started to gibber and staggered off. Such events were frightening.

Bullying was more contained in those days. A playground morality had some restraining influence – that kind of 'don't kick a man when he's down' idea was still in currency.

Miss Holding, a small, lively, Miss Marple-like woman, was fascinating to us boys – she was Queen of the Lurid. A highly religious if morbid woman, she conjured up the most ghastly scenes, from the biblical to the secular, which held us sick with horror – how St Bartholomew was slowly stripped of his skin until his body was the 'colour of this hanky' – here she would let flutter a silky neck scarf the colour of dark magenta – then I was reminded of *Pilgrim's Progress* (once again), how Faithful was burned to death by a howling mob – how Judge Jeffries sentenced prisoners, heavy with chains, to be hung from the gallows – the physical details of the crucifixion of Our Lord and his pain – how last night we bombed Cologne to bits – millions killed – did we read the paper this morning? – the Cathedral's *gone*! How Guy Fawkes could barely sign his name after torture.

The Venerable School Masters were most ancient and quiet pedagogues in their threadbare chalky gowns, reeking of tobacco smoke and pipe shag – ancient because the younger teachers were at the War, but the ones that taught us now had, in some cases, fought in the previous Great War.

Of those immensely long, panoramic photographs depicting a whole school, I have only one – yes – here is the Parade of the Masters, in 1941, and here is one who was in France during the First World War. He was said to have a metal plate in his skull and was called 'Brasso' – very gentlemanly, he suffered torments trying to conduct French singing:

'Right, everybody, *right*!'

> Frerer Jackher
> Frerer Jackher
> Doormeyvoooo
> Doormeyvoooo
> Sunnylegmatiner

Sunnylegmatiner
Bingbangbong
Bingbangbong
BING BANG BONG
BING BANG BONG
Bing Bang *Quiet* Bing
Bing Bang BONG Bing
Quiet Bang Bong *Quiet*

'Shut up and *sit down sit down sit down sit down sit down…*'

Here was Sleepy Nelson, suffering from perpetual somnambulance – his wife looked hot stuff, though, and she was wide awake, it was said – I don't think he noticed the melée swarming about him or the Kipps Apparatus playfully turned on and issuing such a deal of stinking sulphurated hydrogen that we choked and he woke up. The opposite was the unmarried Curly Hughes – rather wild, windy and Welsh, who had been seen in town with a *woman*! Then Mr Mounsey – I called him 'the trench man from Wipers!' – Dougie Young – the kindly zealot and lay preacher – all schools have one. We devoted a little chant to him: 'DOUGAYUNG'S GOTTA BIG FAT BUN!' George Moss – Boy Scout leader, dib dib dib. 'Who is that *boye*??!' 'Toss' Lees – I have long pondered on the meaning of this elderly teacher's sobriquet but, be that as it may, this history master hated me for my long and greasy hair, which I got away with. All decent artists had to have long hair in those days, like Disgustus John, as we cheekily called him.

We all had to be in the Cadet force, unless you were a Boy Scout. 'What did you do in the cadets, Purdy?' I was in the air cadets and Mr Lees, the history master, said we could each have a flight in a Tiger Moth at nearby Sywell aerodrome. I put my name down for it, but he said I could go only if I had a short back and sides – which I did… I looked like a cross between Saint-Exupéry and Amy Johnson. Nobody told me that you have to wear the protective goggles, supplied, if you didn't want your eyes blasted and blinded in the slipstream issuing into an open cockpit. Mine sat unnoticed on my forehead.

Pug Richmond was, as you might guess, of portly build and pinkish hue and one of those long-serving masters who had grown into teacherdom over the weary years and seemed to float above the lessons, disseminating information and brooking no disciplinary obstructions as the mathematics gently poured out of him – calculus, logs, trig, geometry, pi r squared – and in any right-angled triangle – if you didn't get it you didn't get it – I didn't get it. It drifted over me until the bell jolted me upright.

Mr Richmond presided over the Stamp Club, which I attended. He had a superb collection, sections of which he would bring in to show us. The stamps were handsomely affixed with 'mounts' and were written up with copperplate calligraphy, which he also employed on writing our reports.

'Sarki' Johnson, the sarcastic English master, became partially deaf serving with the artillery. This made him irritable. He would suddenly bop a quick fuse, go white with inner anger, stop teaching and make us all fold our arms. If I'd been naughty, I felt slightly guilty because I respected him. I would try to goad him with highfalutin questions about Rimbaud and Baudelaire. He still hung on to Palgrave's *Golden Treasury*.

Essays were being handed in one day and, glancing at mine, Sarki said, 'Adams always tries to shock me!' My piece had commenced, 'The camel was on fire and the green thunder was dripping in the red tower.'

In the minutes before the master arrived in the classroom, whilst keeping my eyes skinned, I was in the habit of chalking on the blackboard enigmatic and opaque messages like, 'The glass dog: I'll be there' and 'What's going on in Africa?' Several blackboard messages throughout the school, which had not yet been rubbed clean in the course of duty, would still linger on the board, inscribed with my 'sayings for the day' to enrich my schoolfriends' lives. The masters, anticipating this, would enter the classroom and cry, 'Wipe that stuff off the board, Adams, and take a detention.' I began to collect detentions, which were useful times for knocking off one's homework.

One or two of the boys were interested and there evolved a fashion for this arcane language, which is not to say there wasn't plenty of derision. Once a boy was jeering at me, and York B. of 5A (or was it Watton M. of 5A?) said, 'Leave him alone! You don't understand him.'

The poor are always with us!

Occasionally, during tuck-time, I would find myself taking on the whole playground. My interest in acting was dangerously spilling over into real life, and what started as a bit of fun became crystallised into little playlets inspired by the comic-strip genre where the communication is through key words such as 'Argg!', 'Wump!', 'Grrr!', 'Howl', 'Slump', 'Pow!', 'Wow!' (the American influence here.) In the corner of the playground, near the bicycle sheds and coal dump, I began to attract an audience idly munching its mid-morning doughnuts. Often I would be gesticulating wildly. Looking up I could see one or two masters looking down from their common room. I couldn't distinguish whether they were amused, censorious, or just pitying. A prefect would be sent along muttering vague threats to clear the decks and, by then, the bell would be ringing for resumption of academic study and I would be back at the desk, exhausted.

My form master, Pug Richmond, took me aside one day and asked me if I was one of these 'Futurists…'

'A surrealist, sir, actually,' I said.

'Why don't you act a bit more manly, Adams? You're becoming the butt of the form.'

'The butt of the *school*, sir, very occasionally,' I suggested.

Sex

And what about sex as we know it?

Besides my attraction to Mimi – ethereal, innocent – the wellsprings of sex later sought expression in the school library each week.

A 'certain type of boy' would go straight to a certain shelf where the fat encyclopaedia sat (not to be removed from the library) and the senses could feast upon an almost explicit portrayal of Adam and Eve in the nude, except for some decorous tresses.

One could then turn from the holy to history and appreciate a study of Lady Godiva (nudish), which could be found on page 261 of the *Harmsworth Self Educator*, Volume 2. Shame, indeed, on he who would turn and peep at her who could save great Coventry from the turmoil of its taxation troubles.

Meanwhile, untoward activities were taking place in the darkest recesses of the library. While the teacher sat at a desk, checking, taking in and stamping out scrofulous books, some of us in the third year would indulge in 'horseplay' and chase each other in and out of the shelves and shadows, grabbing each other's genitalia... It came to be known as 'balling'.

The Female Principle had not emerged in our psyches and I would have to wait until I joined the art school.

Further on parade was Parrot Jones – no parrot, but more an owl perhaps, who was in charge of Latin.

Penates ad larem suum reverti viriplaca deverra Picumnus (if I might put it that way).

(Writer's note: I don't know what this means – could it be canine Latin? – but it has been inserted here with respect to, and on behalf of, Parrot, who doubtless would have known what it meant.)

Parrot was said to disappear at lunchtime in search of nunc est Bibendum (know what I mean?). Through long, sleepy afternoons he was responsible for introducing to us the archaic antics of Julius Caesar, tangling with the Gauls up the Alps.

There was also the nameless teacher who got two years for indecency in 'Stinker's Avenue' swimming baths. If a boy had forgotten his bathing costume he was told to jump in naked as a punishment, to a barrage of giggles.

'You know, it's perfectly natural to be naked – nothing to be ashamed of,' said the teacher, his eyes lighting up.

Elderly Ben Swindon, who was simply just there, was as mild as maths itself, a perfect gentleman. He whispered, sotto voce, when communicating. No boy ever thought of misbehaving in his class. His presence was almost mystical.

'Dickie' Richardson Jones

'Dickie' Richardson Jones was the music teacher at the Grammar School, and organist and choir master at the town's main church, All Saints.

He was a short, tubular man who led us slowly through classical minstrelsy, Mendelssohn, but mostly Schubert: 'Hark, Hark the Lark at Heaven's Gate Sings and Phoebus 'gins to rii-ghh-zizer', and the unfortunate choice of 'Where the Bee Sucks There Suckeye…', which can be modified by altering one letter of a certain word that will make it, frankly, nay, franker and fruitier, in meaning, which we rude, gruff songbirds appreciated. Dickie couldn't understand the giggling that always seemed to accompany this piece.

He served in the cavalry during the Great War – apparently he would never talk about his experiences, as was the case with some of the other teachers. He had a certain quiet reserve. His son, Keith Richardson Jones, later became a lifelong friend after we met at the Art School.

Mr Richardson Jones was the composer of the 'School Song', which I print here for your delectation. The words were by my earlier Headmaster, Mr W. C. C. Cooke, known as 'Pimp' or 'W.C.', a corpulent buffer and one of the old school who left soon after I had begun my time there. W. C. C. Cooke's grasp of verse left a lot to be desired as expressed in these stanzas:

The School Song

> When Thomas Chipsey made this School
> In fifteen forty one,
> Not for his gain or pride he sought,
> But for Posterity he wrought,
> Thus was our work begun.
>
> *Chorus:*
> When the day seems long and the work goes wrong,
> When the wisest seems a fool,
> There's a song we'll sing, till the rafters ring,
> Long live the good old School.
>
> Now centuries have rolled away,
> Northampton's fame spreads wide,
> But all discerning folk will own,
> Who bred the men who made her known,
> And hail the School with pride.

> We've playing fields where boys may learn
> The rules that make the game;
> Those rules that guide the mimic strife,
> Control the sterner game of life,
> And point the way to fame.
>
> With eager heart and mind we face
> The problems of our day;
> Oh, boys must come and boys must go,
> The School remains for ever so,
> Once more we'll raise our lay.

I remember tears in Mr Cooke's eyes when he conducted his last assembly in front of the school. As we quietly marched off, subdued, in our ranks, we small boys were heard to say amongst ourselves, almost reverently, '…did you see Old Pimp? He was blubbing – did you see?' 'I feel kind of sorry for him, really…' We broke up for the hols earlier that day. W. C. C. Cooke's era had come to an end.

The Ramblers Acting Company

'Adams! Go to the foyer of the theatre, find Mr Bascomb and say to him, "Mr Bascomb, I want to be an actor."'

This was to be realised some twelve years later, and it was the ever-inspiring Miss Holding that uttered the above command, but I didn't know what a foyer was. Ten or so of us boys had got together to put on plays. Our troupe and I had just 'brought the curtain down' on our performance of a shrunken 'Midfunny Night's Dream' (the funny bits), our scenery the dark glades, that lay like Dunsinane, at the bottom of 'Bigside' school playing fields. Our audience comprised Miss Holding, the merry Mr Young, some stray masters who happened to be passing by, a pack of cubs and a gang of scouts. (Our 'Wall' character was a scout called Purdy M., who went on to make a name for himself as a missionary in the Baptist stew of Wythenshaw.)

I have forgotten how we got the press interested. I think Miss Holding asked them to come to see another performance after school. As noted in the newspaper, our performance was achieved 'without the knowledge or help of the teachers'. For some months previously I had de-constructed myself and re-emerged as Sir Donald Wolfit, allowing myself the best parts in our productions. In this one I was, of course, Bottom the Weaver. We launched this same production in a Baptist Hall, after some insider chapel chicanery by 'Wall' (the Lord have mercy on him for this), with the addition of the Miss Patsy Barratt School of Dancing in a fairy ballet, complete with Titania, played by the sister of one of the actors. During the performance I mistakenly pushed on stage, ahead of time, the Baptist 'Wall', who, thus locked within his ungainly avant garde à la Picasso cardboard costume, found himself wandering the boards looking hopelessly lost, bumping into the fairy folk's entrechats and seriously scattering the choreography. But we had a proper stage, curtains and blue and orange footlights at last. We had become 'big'.

Some months before this we had formed the 'Ramblers Acting Company' and had performed six plays in the gymnasium and classrooms, often encouraged by Mr Young – hallelujah. These plays were published by a firm called Abel Heywood and Company – terrible stuff that could be performed without paying royalties. We had opened with a thriller entitled 'When the Picture Falls'. As scripted, the falling of the picture was a frightful omen. The trouble was we could never get it to fall on cue. Or even to fall.

Once we set up the show in my mother's bedroom and performed our play to her. Already she was bed-bound with sclerosis. I remember her signalling to us that she much appreciated it.

Before this, when still younger, I had created a little dream theatre in a room of the house – the only spare room available – and fixed up, with my baby brother's help, a curtain of blankets, an extra light or two and scenery painted on large sheets of brown paper with distemper colours. Unfortunately, I didn't know that, to make the colour permanent, one had to mix the powder paint with size glue to fix it; thus a mess of variegated powder gradually flaked off all over the room, much to my father's chagrin. There was capacity for five punters in the audience and one place for a personage working as prompter, stage manager and special effects (including ghosts).

This, surely, was one of the first examples of 'Fringe Theatre' as we know it. Today we take our theatre as it comes – from the Palladium to a dirty room where one squirms on pews – always pews. Due to the decline of religion, the Church of England has been off-loading its pews, which are then bought up cheaply by left-wing idealists to furnish tiny theatres, in order to spread subversion of the Body Politic.

'Tabula rasa'

The primitive gestural acts of scribbling and writing flowed early in my veins – my first 'creative media outlet', as we would call it now.

I must have been ten when I 'published' my own magazine, which I called 'The Rambler', with apologies to the great panjandrum, Dr Johnson, of whom I had not yet heard but whom I later portrayed at the Royal Court Theatre in London and the Traverse Theatre in Edinburgh and wrote a play about. I sold the magazine for 3d per copy to the boys and girls round about 'The Backs' of St James and it was carbon-copied until indecipherable. The contents of 'The Rambler' emulated the style of children's periodicals, with a format like the *Boys' Own* paper, containing puzzles, cartoons, stories, a stamp collectors' corner, advertisements, maps of unknown Treasure Islands... It soon collapsed as it was too laborious to carry out, even though I had help.

I had always been interested in words and writing essays at school, and now began to write stories inspired by some of the books we had at home by H. G. Wells, Dickens, Lewis Carroll, to be found amongst the dross. I was particularly fascinated by the morbid tales of Edgar Allan Poe, not to mention the *Beano* and, for more advanced readers, the *Hotspur*.

I commenced each piece of writing by sketching out the rough pattern of the story on scrap, feint-lined foolscap paper with a Venus green 2B pencil, nicely sharpened, and would transfer the story into a pristine, thick, hard-covered exercise book purloined from the general stock. The story would be laboriously copied out as neatly as possible in Stephen's violet ink or a violent green Quink ink, and even Indian ink, which was found to be too thick and heavy. An india rubber was little used, but the pretty, dusky pink of blotting paper presented a seductive surface and had to be carefully applied to create smudging. The accidental splodges on the blotting paper could remind one of the possibilities of seeing visions in the texture of old walls – battles – landscapes – of which Leonardo da Vinci spoke. The manufacturer of Stephen's Ink was known as 'Inky Stephens'. His laboratory is still in Finchley, protected by the Finchley Society under the aegis of the well-known humorist Spike Milligan.

My most horrifying piece was called 'The Skeleton of the Green Lake'. (Readers may find this story disturbing).

A gentleman comes down from his bedroom one morning and, in happening to look at the French windows, notices the door is slightly ajar and there is a little deposit of green slime on the carpet.

He says to himself, 'That's queer,' and, in going over to examine it, observes that the green slime is in the shape of footprints walking from the lake towards the house. He broods on this horrid phenomenon...

The next morning, having put it all down to a quirk of nature (and previous heavy drinking) like the corn circles the farmers find and explain as the work of fairies, he comes down and sees the window open again and the slimy footprints now making their way towards the *bedroom* – there is an odour of dank, putrescent plankton...

I can't remember what happened next ...and, stoic reader, what about the key...? Was it still used to come in and out of a door?

Would a transubstantiated ghoul bother about a key?!

Miss Cook

I often went to the town library of an evening – an oasis of bookworms, in a brown study. In particular it was the Reference Library, heavy with grey marble and dark panelling, that I loved – the Art Section.

The public and the reference libraries were contained within the Carnegie Hall, the spawn of Andrew Carnegie, the great American philanthropical millionaire who left a trail of munificent edifices for the education of the peasantry throughout the British Isles earlier last century.

Here in Northampton the building also housed a room devoted to John Clare, our local pastoral poet, who went mad and ended his days unknown in the St Andrew's lunatic asylum, which adjoined the grounds of my grammar school. Boys in class behaving badly might be pulled up by their irritable master for their aberrant behaviour and pilloried with the suggestion that they would be better off leaving the classroom and going 'next door'.

As you may imagine, this unpleasantness was sometimes directed at me and, in later years, there was a certain truth in this connection, although I have never been sectioned (as yet).

The building contained a concert hall – I heard Daniel Barenboim and Jacqueline du Pré being angry with each other on the afternoon that I heard them play – and I also heard Richter. The heavily panelled hall was dominated by a huge painting of King Henry II, half naked, about to be flogged and a load of monks standing by. He was about to expiate his sin of being involved in the death of Thomas à Becket, who had connections with Northampton. A peep at this masochistic scene through the concert hall door on one's way to the Reference Library would steel one emotionally for a meeting with Miss Cook – a Brunhilderesque female who controlled behaviour from the moment of entering this erudite domain of hunched figures, absolutely still, in a tableau of frozen postures – encyclopaedists, all hungry for knowledge. A gargantuan sneeze might shake us all up, making us jump.

This Boadicea of the Books would brook no nonsense. She ruled by psychological terror. Stout and fearsome, her eye locked on to you on entry as one hesitantly crept towards a monumental, open tome that had seemingly lain there since time immemorial, as if sacred, on the front desk.

This was the signing-on book – the proof that one was one and no one else. Miss Cook would rise and lumber forth, exchanging a battery of both grunts and greetings. She would then watch and check the ceremony:

Take up pen.

Dip in Quink ink.

Sign name.

TIME of entry.

Questions and Enquiries.
NO BLOTS.
TIME of departure.

When it was established that all papers were in order, permission was given to tip-toe towards the tomes to examine them. Sometimes I liked to browse, but Miss Cook hated readers not being visible and called them to heel. One would be enjoined to make less noise and settle down in some sedentary position with one book. Keeping still was torture. Quiet... Ears grew preternaturally sensitive. Wooden floorboards would involuntarily creak with the worn-out lesions of a century ... the constant turning of pages like the wash of waves ... in the darkest corner what could be lovers were signalling to each other at opportune moments ... the baleful stare of the poet Dryden on a plinth gave notice of his connection with Northamptonshire.

A madman sat hunched over a copy of *Country Life*, planning his next move...

Many years later, I passed Miss Cook in Abington Street. She was very old. As she passed I whispered, 'My library is at your disposal, Madam.'

A film in your front room! – With Pathéscope!

It is hard to appreciate how exciting it was (before the age of the television set) to have an actual movie film in your front room – a palace of dreams.

My father's first projector was the 9.5 Pathé 'Ace', which was cranked by hand. Oh, the romance of an unsteady, flickering picture – the black and white grainy texture – the indecipherable image, the background music on the gramophone, which was effectively wrong – the 'Nutcracker Suite' to Siegfried killing the dragon – the slowing down because of arm fatigue – an abrupt halt. However...

My father cut a hole in the backroom wall and the kitchen became the projectionist's booth, giving a greater 'throw' to the image, and he would slowly serve cups of tea for lack of a bimbo selling ice-creams.

My poor father became obsessed with the technicalities of the 'sport' and might be up much of the night mending, splicing, scraping, joining up the bits of films. I might find him snoring, slumped over a copy of *The Cabinet of Doctor Caligari*.

My father had bought the projector and was borrowing films, which included German classics such as *Metropolis* (we may hear of this later...), *Siegfried, Faust, Donald Duck, Chaplin, Walter Ford, Here Comes the Zoo, The White Hell of Pitz Palu*, the original 'Silly Symphony', *Skeleton Dance, Popeye, Betty Boop*, and, of course, *Caligari*.

Made in 1919, this classic tells a tale through the eyes of a madman, backed by expressionist scenery that wobbled and bizarre acting that was 'ober die topf'. Of course, this film, depicting a homunculus that is brought to life by a weird doctor, is much related to the creature that appears in *The Rocky Horror Show*.

Inevitably there could be times when the projected film became a 'disaster movie' and the tiny audiences would start tapping their tiny feet – luckily it was a carpeted floor.

Would the film behave itself or would it end in tears? The home movie kit was a temperamental one and had a built-in wilfulness that could frighten a projectionist if he didn't keep his wits about him or had neglected to study the operative manual.

'Hullo! Lights! Quickly, please! Never mind the cup of tea! *Lights*! Aagh! Whoops! Something's gone wrong.'

The projectionist often found himself knee-deep in fast-spooling film spinning free like the black nitrate intestines of an alien curling up his leg and escaping into the audience – and munching.

A similar occurrence can happen when the film starts juddering as it jumps out of the 'gate' and rollocks off at a tangent, spewing up huge loops of celluloid.

Sometimes the film will misalign itself and the two sprocket claws jump slightly and start punching two white blobs into the middle of the picture, tearing mercilessly at the cellular surface.

The greatest horror is when the film suddenly stops of its own volition and the picture frizzles and fries before your eyes, accompanied by an odour of burning.

A lamp explodes: *phutt*!

My baby brother got caught by the bug and ran a company called 'Mobile Movies' that would deliver a film show on your doorstep anywhere in Northamptonshire. The rise of television gradually sank this. The poor child was mad about movies.

Music

The self-produced entertainment from the school was conventional. Every Christmas we would break up to the sound of Gilbert and Sullivan. It was amusing to see the masters acting, revealing a part of themselves that was severely repressed. Entertainments were few and far between. A grammar school was not meant to spend too much time on the Arts when it should be parsing or grappling with litotes.

Once there was a pianoforte recital by a lady in the school hall – very unusual. Suddenly Latchford W. 'trumpeted with his rump' (as Rabelais puts it) in the middle of the more delicate resonances of 'Clair de Lune'. The row of boys in the vicinity rocked and heaved with scarce-suppressed mirth. This explosive expression of gaseous exhalation is still, even today, de trop in our

John as a baby.

Portrait in oil of John as a child by G. H. B. Holland, an artist friend of John's father.

A Christmas card drawn by John's father (*left*) while a prisoner of war for four years in Munster Prison Camp, Germany, during the First World War.

Opposite above and below left Three self-portraits as an art student.

Below right A portrait of Elisabeth Frink painted by Jonathan while at Chelsea Art College.

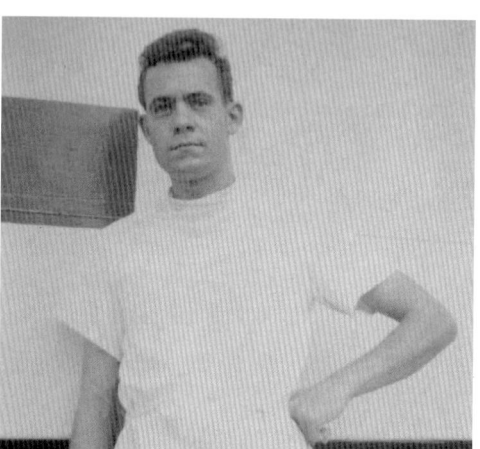

Above and left National Service days in Penang as a Medical Orderly.

Below Jonathan doing his one-man show in Penang, 1954.

COLLAGE OF A LIFE

Above Flying home after National Service.

Left Jonathan as the Narrator in the Royal Court production of *The Rocky Horror Show*.

Below Jonathan as Dr Johnson in *Heaven and Hell* at the Royal Court Theatre.

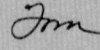

> 5th June 1980
>
> Dear Jonathan —
>
> Now that it's too late to turn back, I wanted to write a brief fan letter to thank you for all that your unique and delightful comic talents have brought to the show. I cannot overestimate your versatility, which has brought out things in the songs that even I hadn't realized were there. It has been a pleasure watching your demonstrations of gentle insanity, and I shall miss seeing you perform.
>
> Best of luck to you, both in this show and in the future.
>
> With gratitude and affection,
>
> Tom

Above and left A letter from Tom Lehrer after the opening of *Tom Foolery* at the Criterion Theatre, London, with a programme signed by the whole company.

Below A production of David Pownall's *Master Class* at the Old Vic, with (l-r) Timothy West as Stalin, Peter Kelly as Prokofiev, Jonathan as Marshal Zhdanov and David Bamber as Shostakovich.

A leaflet for Jonathan's one-man show *The Happy Hour*.

Jonathan playing the piano in his one-man show.

VIII   Collage of a Life

Above Jonathan painting on holiday in Bali.

Right Jonathan painting in Penang, 1981.

Below Joan and Jonathan on holiday in Greece.

society, be it polite society or even that of the lumpen proletariat. And the concert carried on.

Another school concert/revue I attended featured a selection of banal items: 'I'm riding along on the crest of a wave' sort of thing and 'Down at the ferry boat inn everybody's making merry!'. It also included a rendition of 'Oh for the Wings of a Dove' by Mowlem G. of 4B. His ethereal 'piping treble' effect – like the famous Ernest Lough recording – moved me so much that I returned the next night to hear it again. I remember on days following that I wanted to be near him, like a kind of groupie, as we speak of them these days.

A few days later in the playground, having just performed a ritual, I was nearby when Mowlem G. brought out a knife and 'swanked' with it to a few boys in a dangerous manner, injuring one of them. Blood spilled. He was hauled before the new Headmaster. Apparently, Mowlem G. had been playing truant. He was beginning to get a name as a ne'er-do-well.

One morning at the end of assembly the new Headmaster stated in an abrupt manner, 'A boy has been expelled for truancy. His name is Mowlem.'

He swept off the stage. The hush was tangible and the disturbing effect took time to wear off. Storm clouds were gathering. The school was said to be deteriorating from its 'Manners Maketh Man' mould. The new Headmaster had arrived to sort things out – M. B. 'Stinger', BA…

Stinger was six and a half feet tall and like a gorilla on a short fuse. If he was coming towards you along the passage you beat it, or he'd beat you. Handsome and a devotee of the maintenance of physical health, be inaugurated mass morning PT (now called PE). To the clang of a bell, the whole school changed into vests and shorts at the double and assembled in the playground rather in the manner of Mao's workers in Tiananmen Square or a Reifensthal rally. Being forced down into a bending position behind a mate, one saw some unholy sights.

The proceedings were conducted by an old boy called Cadman, indeed a cad, who had a swanky swagger about him. My baby brother reported that he was also to be seen whipping up the 'Minors of the ABC' on a Saturday morning as they sang their club anthem at the Exchange Cinema and then settled down to a Roy Rogers feature. The spirit of J. Arthur Rank was omnipresent. Cadman was obviously a Parade mover and shaker.

One or two of us didn't take kindly to this collective muscle-bashing. Failing rain and storm, we found a way to slope off to cower from this health threat under a distant bush, read poetry and then re-emerge when the bell tolled.

This was a similar strategy to the one we employed on cross-country runs. My friend, Michael Jones, a natural clown but with more intelligence and academic prowess than myself, later became a purveyor of jewellery and a shaker and mover of ecclesiastic forays in the town. Jones M.'s house was on the direct route of the run. We would set off in our kit and very slowly 'run' towards his house nearby, slip inside and settle down for an educational afternoon with J. S. Bach. An hour later, when we saw the first of the runners stagger by, sticky and sweating, we would let most of them pass before ambling out to join the main team, feigning exhaustion.

It behoved one not to be late because the last runner would be seized and have his pants pulled down.

One day poor Jones M., however, suffered the full weight of 'The Sting' and it was not altogether his fault. He received six of the best from Stinger for connivance in trying to erase the evidence of an entry of his name by Sleepy Nelson in the detention register. A lout called Carter J. also received six for the same misdemeanour. It was actually he that bungled the rubbing out. It was plain to see that someone had interfered with the register. The lout had executed a kind of soft-shoe shuffle on the page, which left it looking muddy and distressed.

Jones M. was biting back the tears when he came out into the playground where we were waiting for him to ask how he'd got on.

Stinger had a unique arrangement for processing supplicants that called at his study, be they boys, masters or parents.

Pressing a bell activated one of three illuminated panels, thus:

COME IN
WAIT
GO AWAY

A swimming pool was built in the grounds and, if Parents' Day turned out hot, he was in the habit of stripping off, diving in and executing some aquatic dithyrambics, clambering out and talking nonchalantly about the 11+ to the guests in his dripping trunks.

On my last report he wrote, 'I congratulate him warmly on his excellent acting and even more so on the initiative he displays over it. A promising artist with the usual academic shortcomings. He should become a great actor or artist.'

Some are born great. Some have greatness thrust upon them. I don't know what happened to mine, but it's too late now.

'Stinger's last years were overclouded by the proposals to turn the school into a comprehensive institution. He was a believer in the value of the Grammar School. He tried to "save" the school but the effort was too much for him. It brought on a nervous breakdown, which led to his death in tragic circumstances during the Easter holidays in 1964.'

(from *A Short History of Northampton School for Boys* by T. C. Lees)

Amateur dramatics

Only recently I was passing the Doddridge Chapel hall in St James and thought I'd peer in to where I first started amateur dramatics fifty years ago and where the Boys' Brigade held their palavers and scouts their jamborees.

As I remember it, the hall was a morose chocolate brown, a grubby place typical of chapels and church halls up and down the country, but it could turn into a world of magic when the lights dimmed and the tatty dust-charged curtains flopped to the sides revealing an uneasy group of young people, dressed in very-well-made fancy costumes, waiting in trepidation for the first line to be delivered or forgotten and the show to get under way.

Round the corner from me lived Paddy Maguire, an ex-WAAF, later a teacher and amateur actress. She was a member of 'Bottom Dodd' and produced quality religious dramas with adolescents of the chapel. She eschewed sentimental Joseph and Mary saccharine stuff in favour of T. S. Eliot, James Bridie, medieval mystery plays, André Obey's *Noah*. Being so near I was soon leaned on to help as the only 'artist' in St James. I had to do the scenery. I also played Joseph, the third Wise Man on the left, the third shepherd on the right and the Devil. Eventually I was promoted to the role of God. I couldn't go further than that, so prepared myself to move to the adults' world of the amateur Northampton Players when I left school…

Bless my soul! The sound of noisy boys breaks my reverie as I enter the hall. Here are two ageing men parading about in uniform (amidst a group of youngsters), whom I recognise as being boys who were once in class with me. We have a chat. (One or two of the brigade had died but the flag was still flying. The Religious Drama had long dissolved). The hall is exactly the same as it was fifty years ago (if this is a logical distinct possibility). It is about to be pulled down.

I remember the final school months leading into my next four years at the Art School as 'golden' – the smell of mown grass, the bright, white costumes of the cricket players – always far away – pretty, but not an inducement to me to take part – the ring of the bells, the click of balls and the distant cries of 'lbw!' and 'howzat!'.

I seemed to be in the art room more than in the classroom's groves of academe where I was polishing off the few school certificate papers I was capable of taking (1 Art, 1 Science, 2 Religious Knowledge, 2 English Literature – all just passed – but Religious Knowledge – *Credit*! A humbling result for an atheist, God forgive me).

The school celebrated, in this year of '47, its centenary (delayed because of the war) with an historical pageant. I enjoyed painting Ye Olde Scenery of 1541 on huge flats, playing the Prologue and, stuffed with a couple of cushions, Henry VIII.

The pageant was master-minded by the new art teacher, 'Archie' Gommon. After the performance of the pageant, Mr Gommon's wife, who stimulated the cast in the production and was trying to get rid of the Northampton accent among those playing the aristocracy (which completely lacks any dramatic potential), asked me if I'd been nervous. I replied, 'All good actors are nervous, Mrs Gommon.'

In Baxter's day, the art class's favourite demonstration lesson was 'how to draw tanks' – my art contribution was not outstanding and it was only towards the end of my time at school that some inspiration came forth; I began to be aware of 'Modern Art' or 'Futurism', as it was then called, and was fascinated by Picasso's genius. I saw his ferocious, horse-nosed women in a copy of the weekly *John Bull* periodical and began to pour out pastiches of the modern masters – the cubism of Braque, the fairy tales of Klee, the odalisques of Matisse, the sugary lovers of Chagall and horror of Dali.

Mr Gommon gave me great encouragement and allowed me the liberty of experimentation. He hung my pictures all over the school, which often engendered some jeers and scorn. It was over-exposure, flooding the market, so to speak.

That last golden summer I would bicycle over to Little Billing, where the Gommons rented a country dwelling, past the pea-green pickin'-good landscape that I occasionally plucked for a shilling an hour, to eat kippers in the garden, prepared by his madly attractive wife, Jean.

Their charming early-nineteenth-century rectory had only gaslight by which to read. In the summer the house peeled, creaked and grumbled.

Paling in the sun was Mr Gommon's considerable collection of thumbed books by the philosophers, old photos and magazine cuttings, framed, of Beethoven, Socrates, Rembrandt, Spinoza, Goethe, Blake and Baudelaire, hung, slightly askew, on the plastered walls. I called them 'The Old Boys'. Heartening sayings by William Blake were painted on the walls in distemper.

On a hot afternoon I would leaf through these mighty founts of thought and begin to nod off, while, faintly blowing in the distance were, not the horns of elfland, but the chords of Billing's Aquadrome muzak, an early example of theme parking even before Spain was reinvented for holidays.

The garden was a hymn to Delius, bursting with rambling flowers and wild foliage.

Once, my friend Purdy (Wall) and myself dressed up as Bengalis and cycled over to see the Gommons. Slowly we perambulated into the long front garden and observed that Mrs Gommon (may I call her Jean now?) was busy near the potting shed with her trug. We introduced ourselves in a 'furrin' gentlemanly manner but Jean seemed to sense something untoward and said that she'd go in to get her husband. This she soon did and he came out. The truth soon became apparent. We were not offered kippers.

Just a little kipperesque story.

David Gommon's paintings had about them something of the poet – drawn from the pastoral school of Samuel Palmer. He continued to find mystery in an ever-declining Northampton and his front garden. He was a visionary pursuing a lonely path. His comparative lack of recognition was perhaps due to his diffidence. He is one of those who will be fêted in later years.

Purdy (Wall) remembered being on our lawn one hot autumn day, lounging in the last blaze of sunlight, lazily regarding the floral hanging-baskets, the wisteria, not unlike the purple and violet 'Orbiston' colours, the proliferating honeysuckle creeping across the veranda, covering it fulsomely, the garden with its carefully constructed rockeries laid out by my father – he never quite finished his projects – and the apple tree he would laboriously plunder for the always bird-pecked, insect-ridden fruit whilst balancing up a rattling ladder. My baby brother played with the remains of our decrepit perambulator, which became his 'bus'.

Purdy (Wall) remembers my mother sitting inert in her dressing-gown in an armchair by the window, exuding inexpressible loneliness, looking into the hot garden, as pale as a ghost in the shadows of the late afternoon. Inevitably, and very slowly, she would lean helplessly over to one side and have to be righted, like a ship.

My father had suddenly noticed her body through her nightgown and he decided there and then to abandon her medically prescribed spartan regimen. Every evening my father had concocted a salad that he attempted to arrange as edibly and attractively as possible.

My mother might giggle a little to people we met as I gave her an outing in the wheelchair round Harlestone Road, Dallington, or a large housing estate that was being built nearby. Indeed, the first time that my father knew there was something amiss was when in bed she would giggle for no reason. From then on she deteriorated with sclerosis and my father looked after her basic needs whilst continuing his job at the factory and caring for my brother and I. He was demoted because he couldn't cope and would take home the tide of figures and sums that engulfed him. So weighty did he feel his task that I heard him once say, 'I wish I could die.'

His trial was to end. The 1947 winter was as vicious as any felt in former years. The country was paralysed. Snow-drifts were seven feet high. My brother and I could hardly get to school or my father to his factory.

My mother suddenly suffered a major stroke, which was not unexpected: She lay in bed and, three days later, died. The snow drifts lay heavy on the morning of her death.

As I began to wake up I heard the sound of low voices in my parents' room. Dr Traylen had certified death and the body was being laid out in a frilly shroud. After a time our father called us in. We stood for some time in our dressing-gowns not showing much overt emotion with father standing there. Then he suggested we leave the room and get dressed. Later he observed that I hadn't shown much response to seeing mother on her death bed. I went into the lavatory and wept.

5
Art School

G. H. B. Holland

We had in the town those whom we used to nickname 'the Triumvirate', elderly artists who had settled for ever in Northampton.

George Herbert Buckingham Holland – GHB for short (not GBH) – was a bearded portrait-painter who was a friend of my father. He taught my father the craft of etching with the help of a Mr Kyte. My father had bought a giant etching press and I heard them all at it well into the night as I went to sleep. He produced some fine topographical scenes of Northampton.

GHB painted a portrait of me when I was about seven years of age. As I sat for it I was grumpy and kept aligning my nose away from his vision. GHB tempted me with chocolate. I didn't like being looked at. Too much chocolate was becoming sickly. He attempted to keep me awake with small jokes.

Undeniably, I was emerging in the portrait as a glamour puss: the lips were a little too rosy, the hair too threadgold and curly; my eyes too bright and melting and the blue sky a little too sky blue, with the skin as delicate as a baby's bottom.

There is no doubt that I was a beautiful child, according to the photographs of myself that I have obsessively amassed throughout the years. Apparently, people used to stop my parents in the street and say, 'Oh, my! What a beautiful child, m'duck.'

Do you find this talk too kind of fulsome? Turn over if so.

I was talking to my beautician the other day and, while discussing the date of my next appointment, she vouchsafed the opinion, 'You're no oil painting, you know.'

'You're wrong,' I gainsaid. 'I was done in oils when I was seven by GHB, my good woman!'

GHB confirmed this in later years and indeed I own the work in question.

Just before he died he told me that my mother and father were not at ease together, my mother being practical and not at all imaginative whilst my father was 'artistic' and 'dreamy'.

Tom Osborne Robinson

The theatre scenic designer at the Northampton Repertory Company was Tom Osborne Robinson, known as Tom. He spent all his life in the town and died in it, completing fifty years' work at the theatre. He was a major patron and benefactor of Northampton Museum and Art Gallery who undertook commissions for the Old Vic, the RSC, and lectured here and in the USA. He was born in the town and maintained a great love for the place.

Tom was a tireless campaigner for the arts as the town around him slowly started being torn apart by the planners who went to work in the sixties, and he spent his life fighting for the remains of what character was left. I saw him, one fateful morning, witnessing the pulling down of the monumental Victorian fountain in Market Square. The council insisted that this tough iron structure was unsafe but, as dusk fell, the demolition crew still hadn't been able to topple it, so strong was it. I swore I saw tears in Tom's eyes as we watched the ironwork split and buckle, in eventual submission to the dismantlers. He pleaded for a piece of the ironwork from the workmen. An elegant shopping arcade was the next to go – another loss in a market square that Tom felt to be one of the best in Europe. Half of it is no more.

Tom was a quietly spoken man, almost mumbly in conversation, which belied the swagger of his inner romanticism. He dressed extravagantly, rather in the manner of a Venetian gondolier. He was enthusiastic about Venice. If he could work a bit of Venice into the set that week, even if it was one for an Agatha Christie thriller set in the Home Counties, he would do it. Another sartorial extravagance he sported was one that came dangerously near to that of a teddy boy – drainpipes, super-enlarged coat, string knotted tie, striped socks and winkle-pickers, but all in exquisite taste.

His sets were highly esteemed nationally until the advance of minimalist black rostra, with actors sharply delineated in bright light or a colourless void. No actor could grab the limelight with Tom's sets around, which were vigorously executed, brightly coloured, modernistic, semi-cubist, exuberant extravaganzas, all slapped on in a week! When the curtain rose, there would be admiring applause.

What sheer hard work were the days of weekly Rep, for the designers as well as the actors. Tom tried to build up the local art collection to some quality. I must confess he bought one of my 'Rotting Cathedral' series for the town, but the last time I saw it exhibited was twenty-nine years ago. Presumably it is still rotting in the museum vaults below.

Tom was also a teacher at the Art School on Fridays. Two of his pupils were Champion and Pidcock.

Henry Bird

The third of the Triumvirate, Henry Bird, was reared 'neath the shadows of the gasworks and gained something of a reputation as a bright student at the Royal College of Art. I seem to discern the quality of a Stanley Spencer in his earlier pictures.

The only one of the Big Three to leave Northampton, for a time, he settled in Oxford and London and married the actress Freda Jackson, who was playing at the Rep. Henry designed sets for the Embassy Theatre, Swiss Cottage, Sadlers Wells and the Old Vic, and impressive safety curtains for Northampton Repertory Theatre and the Ashcroft Theatre in Croydon.

While I was still at Northampton School of Art, Henry returned to the fold of his birth and obtained a teaching post at the school. I didn't altogether see eye-to-eye with him sometimes. His style had moved to a sort of pre-Raphaelite imagery, meticulously wrought. The likeness of his wife, Freda, could be detected dominating the dancing, swirling figures in a Rite of Spring. Drawings of nubile nudes, executed in coloured chalks on tinted Ingres paper, were his metier in later years.

As a student I found myself consigned to painting in the details of one of Henry's murals, in the traditional manner of an apprentice and his master in Renaissance times, touching up the finger nails on a Madonna whilst the master nodded off in the corner.

Every week I would enter school, inflamed from my outpatient treatment for acne, and be employed to execute, in Brodie and Middleton's scenic distemper colours, the embroidery on the knickers of the Dame of the Camellias who had crept into Henry's latest safety curtain.

The next day I might be commandeered to grind pure pigment with pestle and mortar, in the manner of Sir Joshua Reynolds and the Old Masters.

I pointed out to Henry that, in these modern times, he could purchase this pigment from a firm called Winsor & Newton, purpose-ground, and all ready for use in a malleable, artist-friendly *tube*.

About this time the River Nene broke its banks and visited its waters upon those of us dwelling in this low-lying land. The floods swirled from as far as the LMS railway station and goods yard to almost reach the portals of our drawing-room from where I used to watch the Passing Parade.

Now I witnessed the fields of St James (Jimmy's End) transformed into a Water Wonderland – a Venetian 'scena' – complete with cloth-capped lumpen gondoliers plying their floating crafts of rescue and succour.

The shoe factories (pride of Northampton), designed by Victorian architects in red-brick Venetian Palazzo classico style, looked serenely romantic on this particular evening as the sun began to set as in a painting by Turner ... the bus depot had now become an island in the Nene, illuminated flame-red.

'The Nude and its Place in Polite Society'

There was no arguing.

'Go back to your allotment, Dad!' The future would be spent for the next four years as a model dissident student at Northampton School of Art.

David Gommon had given me a 'brilliant' report, suggesting that this was my path to enlightenment. My father and I cycled one evening up the hill they call steep, to the Art School, to discuss this future of mine with the professors therein. Would there be any Bohemianism on the course? Was one allowed a beard? Had they heard of Surrealism?

When we arrived, my father looked white and ill; it was the beginning of heart trouble. (Nevertheless, he lived until the age of eighty-six.) We still managed to discuss my situation and I was accepted as a full-time pupil starting the following term.

Although, technically, still at the Grammar School, I started to attend life classes in preparation for when I joined full time, but it emerged that I was considered to be in the wrong class, as so often happened, until finding my level. They assumed I was more interested in the Saturday morning 'kids' class, which I didn't want as I had given myself only a year to join polite society.

I told my father what had happened and he assumed that I had been removed from the life class in case I should be overwhelmed by the sight of too much rampant female flesh.

Strange tales, taboos and myths circulated about 'what goos on oop there a' th' arschool, m'duck!'

Purdy (Wall) told me that he knew for a fact that the female models posed behind a very large sheet of plate glass so that a decent distance could be maintained between student and model. It would act as an emotional deterrent and prevent overheating, or so he said. I found that this was at odds with verity, as we came to know it.

The affair was sorted out, my father confirming that I was erotically stable, and I was put back amidst the flesh.

My sexual situation discussed here, however, was obviated when the female model (a voluminous bit of fluff) immediately fell ill. When I next reported in to the life class she had been replaced by a male model of unparalleled obesity.

The nude has always had to be policed. The state can collapse when too much nudity is released in society. Except perhaps in Tonga.

It has oft been hinted that in Hampstead there is a swimming pool hidden amidst dense verdure, which is exclusively appointed for women in the nude.

I lived in Hampstead for many years and I must say that, after diligently searching on long Sunday walks for this erotic grove, and feigning the image of a sexless male professor, wearing horn-rimmed glasses, I never found it. I was too embarrassed to ask anyone where it was or even if it still existed. Certainly, the nearby Salvation Army centre wasn't at all helpful, nor was the Women's Liberation group on Downshire Hill.

Continuing this veritable nude theme park (while we're here), it so happened that when I was playing in *The Rocky Horror Show* I was the Equity Deputy (the Trades Union Representative), and the organiser lady from the Equity office asked me to tell the company to wait after the show as she wanted to speak to us.

The lady arrived at our unisex collective dressing room, as it had become, to find the cast already there, removing their costumes and besporting themselves entirely nude, or 'in the nude', except for me, who was caught out that night wearing droopy drawers.

Seeing that she was a little shaken, I asked her if she would feel more comfortable if she took off her clothes, but she declined. Everyone was in a hurry to get home.

'Speak the speech,' we prayed her, 'hurriedly!' which she did and departed.

The next day she telephoned me at the theatre (or rather converted cinema) and I told her that the cast had, for some time now, gone native, but that Plouviez and I were monitoring the situation carefully, watching for any of the cast that might be tempted to go Ape.

She said that as long as the members of the cast were not being pressurised into exhibiting their nude bodies, Equity 'wouldn't object'. I said there was no pressure being applied as far as I knew, excepting myself; I was suffering acute pressure from my Alexander Technique practitioner, but, not to worry, I remained fully clothed for this.

The following week I reported for an audition at the Royal Court Theatre – not for an Equity Rep, but to be considered for the part of a Roman soldier in a farce called *The Romans in Britain*, which was to commence touring Britain. It was by Howard Brenton and was to be followed with a light tragedy *Some Like It Nude*, a more pivotal work.

Who should be there but the Equity lady who had previously met the 'Rocky Horror' actors. Apparently she was still on the lookout for nudes and was conducting a survey on nudity under pressure in Britain, thus checking out whether this Roman soldier would be designated as partially nude or quite nude, give or take a few leather thongs. The general contractual statement pertaining to this show was to classify it as 'NUDE' or 'Nudish'. Mention should be made here of an example of up-front nude wrestling performed by Alan Bates and the bohemian film actor Oliver Reed in *Women in Love* – not the kind of activity one wants in one's dressing room.

This, of course, all happened years ago when nudity on stage and screen was rarely, or barely, seen, and Equity was trying to make sure that its members were not being exploited.

The Reverend Hussey

There lived, in a manse, in the upper ecclesiastical reaches of Northampton, a maverick priest, Canon Walter Hussey. Besides his episcopal duties he was a shaker of la bella arte and a mover of ars musica, besides being vicar of St Matthew's, an edifice that yokel locals still call 'Phipps's Fire Escape'. The benefactor, whose monetary donation gave shape to this holy erection, was a rich brewer called Phipps, so this rude title evolved from the sour observation that his generosity was no more than an insurance policy in order to escape the rigours of hell fire. The donation of a whole church to God would then be seen as proper and decent expiation for the sin of brewing strong drink, which at that time was the curse of the working man.

Canon Walter Hussey, a feverish and voluble cleric, bearing on his shoulders the legacy of this moral turpitude, rode a sophisticated path towards putting Northampton on the artistic map. We saw little of greatness in the art gallery or in the Carnegie Hall; it was he who broke through the parochial resistance to 'Modern Art' and commissioned Henry Moore to execute a 'Madonna and Child' and, later, Graham Sutherland's 'The Crucifixion'. He also drew in famous musicians and composers – the singer Kirsten Flagstad and the then boyish Benjamin Britten and Peter Pears. Some of the best organists were employed.

Hussey was generally perceived as being at variance with the town's expectations of a parish vicar. Still at school, I remember the brouhaha that erupted when Moore's work was revealed in 1946. A cause célèbre, the local paper was full of angry and jeering letters, some accusing the priest of blasphemy, written by people who probably hadn't even seen it, like my ever splenetic father, who said that it looked like a footballer. It is now very difficult to comprehend the hostility aroused at the time, for it evokes a sense of serenity and nobility.

The later arrival of Graham Sutherland's 'The Crucifixion' was considered less offensive. Purdy (Wall) and I, having noted time and date in the newspaper, crept into the ecclesiastic vernissage and looked around. I saw the skeletal John Piper pontificating in the midst of the gathering and thought I saw Champion and Pidcock. Purdy (Wall) was offended by the painting so I had to take him out. I was thrilled with the tragic drama and dark, saturated colours, but did note that it had a certain ancestral connection with Grünewald's Isenheim 'Crucifixion'. The Canon sometimes came into the Art School. In talking to him I discovered his knowledge of atheistic British Surrealism and its influence on Moore and Sutherland. I don't think he found much that was experimental in the Art School.

The Canon amassed a fine collection of British modern art, which is now shown in Pallant House, Chichester, where he was laid to rest as a Bishop. Having performed twice at the Chichester Festival in a production of Zola's *Thérèse Racquin* and the musical *Valentine's Day*, directed by Gillian Lynne, I was able to become very conversant with the works in this museum.

I was now settling in at the Art School and was to be seen stiffly pedalling my ancient Raleigh (circa '30s) up and down by the racecourse where my father had camped with Major Mobb's mob en masse before embarking for the Great War. I was dressed in my tight brown suit, inherited from school days, yellow socks and light blue beret and sandals for the winter.

The first generation of ex-servicemen had also arrived with the walking wounded. They had an open field of young fillies to dally with, and there were a few broken hearts. Their comparative sophistication was helpful to their dalliance. We younger students, being only sixteen years of age as yet, were sometimes a 'pain in the ass' to our elders with our noisy pretensions and self-conscious jeu d'esprit.

I tried to percolate my grammar school Dada ways into the gravitas of the Art School and would suffer a sharp rebuff when it got 'too much' – like a clip on the nape.

One innocenti had his head held under running tap water and was told to cool it.

Another was incarcerated in a wicker clothing basket and heaved down the main stairs with much humping and thumping. The Principal suddenly appeared and asked us how we were getting on with our perspective. Champion emerged, flushed, from the basket, laughing insanely. Pidcock slid away.

A cabbage, propelled by an angry student, released from the gravity of its placement in a 'still life', flew across the studio and smashed the lights. The teachers taking extended tea and scones next door in the common room thought they heard a noise.

Having studied the masters, old and new, in the library, I was surprised by the ignorance of students and, sometimes, teachers too. When this intrepid, spotty youth mentioned artists like Samuel Palmer, Max Ernst or Ivon Hitchens the names evoked no response.

A little lecture

Our exam was called the Intermediate Diploma in Design. This was followed by another two years' study of one's own choice – painting, illustration, sculpture, etc – after which most students did another year for teacher training. A student was expected to become proficient in the basics throughout the course.

What were these basics? And what were not?

We weren't taught colour theory uncoupled from representational painting, or formal relationships other than those in architecture, or a course in cultural studies other than the histories of western art.

Art students had to wait until the 1960s for the arrival of the 'Basic Design' course pioneered 'up north' by Victor Pasmore and Harry Thubron in which an analysis of the fundamentals of art was taught in the wake of the Bauhaus of the thirties.

This course may sound like a new form of academism but it provided a structure to build on.

I found it a difficult position in which to be placed – an R. D. Langian 'double bind'. I tried to follow the academic path and to paint and draw 'proper':

> Monday: Life drawing
> Tuesday: Still life or figure composition
> Wednesday: Portrait painting
> Thursday: Perspective or architecture
> Friday: History of art in the Renaissance

We didn't quite get to Cézanne. I was told it would be best to relinquish my fancy ways and learn the conventional art techniques. We were almost back to 'How to draw tanks'.

Dear Dougie Davis, who taught us anatomy and revealed a most repulsive gluteus maximus when demonstrating the workings of the muscles of this area of the body, said to me, when I was getting too fevered about Dali one day, 'Salvador Dali? Bollocks! Now get on drawing that Ileotibial band.'

Mention should be made here of Alicia Boyle, a lively, red-stockinged, acerbic Irish painter who blew many cobwebs away. She taught part-time within the curriculum but opened our eyes and minds to wider horizons.

She made the girls cry.

More than one enchanted evening?

On the lower floor of the Northampton Art School were placed the Occupational Therapists, some of whom would eventually minister in such places as St Andrew's Asylum.

These females were my age and some were immensely beautiful. Many of them boarded in a Victorian Schloss cobbled together in the style of a Bavarian Castle called 'Rheinfelden'. I would look up as I was passing that way in the hope of spying a damozel with long, blonde tresses, ululating to me from a Gothic window whilst practising the art of kunst therapy at an old spinning wheel.

Being carried away by these visions was not helping my grasp of mature sexual reality. The day would come when I would have to confront one of these lovely creatures *in the flesh*, at tea break, or in the bicycle shed.

Which I did.

I was continuing to give performances of 9.5mm home movies to my fellow students while my father dealt with the tea, and thought these entertainments might act as an entrée into the world of occupational therapy. I haunted the Art School corridors handing out programmes, whilst gently humming, and managed to cajole three therapists into attending a performance of Leni Riefenstahl's *The White Hell of Pitz Palu*, which my father projected through the kitchen aperture. Other students of 'our lot' were there as usual, including Champion and Pidcock. That evening some bitchiness directed by one of our number towards a therapist was reported. I banned the offending student for half a term.

Afterwards, I pursued one of the therapists called Woody by dint of telephoning the Rhein Castle and went out with this very nice girl for a very brief time before the romance faded away.

I would have to get to Chelsea before a relationship of more significance could manifest itself. I was beginning to be interested in going to Chelsea Art School.

After some time, I began to look at one fellow student, Jean (female), in a new light. She happened to live opposite the St Andrew's Asylum, which was still being, and forever will be, facetiously recommended by broken teachers as being a suitable retreat in which to maroon delinquent pupils. We began making unconscious signals to each other of which we were scarcely aware, in an almost Freudian way, if you understand me. I don't know how it began, but I was talking about Jean to Purdy (Wall). He was then a trifle saucy and given to rendezvous with girls at the 'Monkey House' of an evening – a park pavilion round which the more raffish ex-pupils of the Grammar School used to gather. He had not taken up the cloth as yet, and suggested that we ask her, with another art school filly, to join us in hailing a United Counties bus and visiting his mother's mouldering caravan, which lay ditched in a dyke in our local Salcey Forest, taking sandwiches and a flask of nourishing cocoa.

I asked the two girls to throw in their lot with us and assured the other girl, Janet, with bright ginger hair, that Purdy (Wall) was a very nice chappie and a bona fide scouter (dib dib dib).

The evening was spent in nervous banter and jolly japes and gigglement, which took on a fraught quality.

Jean went out to sit on the grass some yards away to puff at a Woodbine and clear her head of the torrid atmosphere that had begun to build up.

While Ginger Janet was occupied for a moment, Purdy (Wall) whispered to me, 'Go and sit by Jean and try and hold her hand.'

I tripped and fell out of the caravan with a soft thud. Slowly and gingerly, and now with mud-caked frontage, I wormed my way towards the silent and reflective Jean. It started to rain. I neared her and sat down. I was nervous and began to talk about Rembrandt, his life and times, Jean's mother, Whistler's mother, what is Art?, and many similar disparate themes.

Suddenly the rain splashed down in heavy tropical-type globules and the hand plan had to be abandoned. We rushed for the caravan…

Bit of a bore, really…

Purdy (Wall) didn't seem to be the worse for wear, nor did Ginger Janet. They were dry.

Night must fall and did so. Yes. We thought we'd better get back … and just missed the last United Counties bus, which meant a considerably wet walk back, successfully drowning any romance that might have been ignited.

Or did it?

I walked Jean back to her house, as was correct in those days, and, as we stood at the front gate (the rain having abated), a sudden impulse urged me on. 'Oh, bugger it! In for a penny…' and I touched her breast – with some feeling.

Jean was surprised.

So was I.

'Oh, you are passionate, John…,' she whispered.

'Well, yes, er … you could say that…,' I quivered.

I saw her to her front door, trembling a little.

'Adams has got a girl!' rang out a surprised cry from the 'Monkey House' some days later.

A tentative relationship developed.

Jean was a voluptuous creature, her shyness belying her sensuality. Her eyes peeped out of a fringe of hair.

Mrs Gommon heard of my girlfriend Jean and gave me an eight-part lesson in etiquette to be employed when entertaining a young lady while suffering compulsive tomgaucherie.

'Girls will go for anything in trousers, John,' Jean Gommon said, trying to give me confidence.

'Will they really?' I said, feeling more positive.

Intense preparations were laid with a view to my inviting Jean to the Gommons' house for a meal of kippers (my usual) and putting what I'd learned about etiquette into red-blooded action.

When the evening arrived, Jean was too shy to come.

Later, Jean sent me a letter. 'I am sitting here writing this in the moonlight… I am sorry… Keith has professed a strong liking for me and I hope we…'

Jean had fallen for one of the ex-servicemen.

'Bastard!'

A quartet

Keith, Jean and myself eventually sorted out our emotional problems. They married. I didn't. With a girl called Barbara Turner (sweet Babs) we had evolved into a 'foursome' in the Art School – sometimes tending to be 'know-alls'.

Keith (ex-RAF Singapore) was the natural, but young, éminence grise, and we used to philosophise, into the small hours, about the arts, as we knew them, in his studio at the top of the family house. Eventually we four moved to a ramshackle pub in the cruder part of Northampton and set up a painting studio on the first floor above the bar. Painting portraits was one activity we pursued – as well as others. It was the nearest we got to working in the atmosphere of a rotting atelier deep in old Montmartre.

In reality, we would work over the sound from below of imbibing British mayhem at varying levels; our door might be slowly opened and a sozzled face would appear and then withdraw slowly after apologising with, 'Sorry, m'duck,' or another might enter and, after some incoherent introduction, would wander round delivering a critique of the paintings until gently persuaded to leave.

As befits the arrogance of the young, we four entertained a 'rosta' of floating invisible Aunt Sallies and celebrity punchbags on which we could bounce our beliefs and which could be summoned up and jeered at when heavy in one's cups.

We held, for instance, a deep hatred for the plebeian, almost equine, Sir Alfred Munnings RA and his endless slick pictures of horses with glossy bottoms. I grieve to say that he was an influence on G. H. B. Holland's work. He threatened to have Stanley Spencer, a fellow RA, arraigned before the law on the grounds that his paintings were obscene. This bigoted attack on a fellow artist didn't gain Sir Alfred many friends in the academic pantheon of British Art.

Sir William Russell Flint we execrated even more than Sir Alfred. His favourite subject was the Female Nude, which he painted in watercolour, his subject usually reclining on an unpolluted beach. These were immensely popular at one time.

In spite of their brilliant water-colour technique, when we were in a graceless mood we would harangue them as vulgar products veering on the PORN-ographic.

When no one was looking I must confess to taking in an eyeful if I passed one in a gallery window.

A whited sepulchre is not a lovely thing.

Pietro Annigoni, who tried to keep the Renaissance going in the sixties and painted our Queen in oils (twice), was beyond the pale for his PHOTO-graphic style. In fact, anyone who painted the Queen was beyond the pale.

There is the curious case of the Woman with a Green Face that still returns to haunt us; why was this, not unattractive, woman *green*? She seemingly came from an Asian background. Humanity comes in assorted colours, but green is not one of them, except when vomiting or in a state of illness.

Painted by one called Tcherekabitch (I think), she could be seen in every Bootsiz front window in the land and is even seen now on occasion. Certainly no charity shop should be without one.

There are others of this ilk that we won't mention.

Our favourite modern artists formed a broad church, though lacking in any religious conviction. Our choice was conventional even then: Picasso, Matisse, Bonnard, Vuillard, Klee, Chagall, Braque. Nobody had heard of Kurt Schwitters.

Although loving the above artists, I found myself alone when it came to Surrealism and Dada, which had fascinated me since I was fourteen. The others weren't interested – sometimes even hostile; they 'had it in' for Salvador Dali and condemned Magritte as a damned bad painter.

Of course, we hadn't heard of Jackson Pollock and American 'Abstract Expressionism'. It had hardly heard of itself.

Music

'Classical' music and, particularly, jazz could be on our chopping block.

Jazz at this time was riven by factions, sects and styles: Blues, Boogie Woogie, Revivalists, Trad (Boom), Dixieland, Ragtime, Mainstream, Modern, Progressive, New Orleans, not to mention Be Bop and more…

Keith, having come back from the RAF in Singapore, was steeped in jazz and I was swept along, to some extent, by the narrowing of his parameters, like his hatred of the 'Glenn Miller' sound, swing, and what we heard on the wireless like Ted Heath and his Orchestra. If Paul Whiteman and his orchestra turns up, shut the 100 Club door *now*! *Out*!

Music by 'light' composers like Eric Coates was *irredeemable*.

Only Armstrong, Roll Morton and their type, with *early* Ellington, were allowed in the purist pantheon of the day.

These divisions can still fester in old age.

Here comes the geriatric passing Jazz Parade.

Guys! Stop and look around you. D'you see these old jazz freaks here? They are now old men (few of them women) whom one sees maundering down the street with a gnarled-top walking stick or trying to negotiate a Zimmer frame, fixated in their period. Disco is anathema. These old men are ghosts, diehards from the Trad boom, perhaps. Observe their hardened, quivering lips – they are muttering to themselves 'Be Bop ba doo bidly bop' to a tune that they've forgotten. They were starved of fresh jazz in their youth; no wonder they now look pinched. One must remember that knowledge of jazz in Britain was severely truncated for many years. Our Musicians Union banned, until 1955, the import of American music in order to protect its members. I remember that, while still at school and a member of our Jazz Club, we became excited because we were going to hear Ellington *on the wireless*, that night, from America!

Jazz in those days was a pitiful minority interest. No wonder we felt superior. Jazz craved respectability and has long since achieved it. Sometimes, now, we can't tell the difference between the avant garde of jazz and avant garde of classical (give you a penny if you can tell me which one is classical and which one jazz, mate).

Ellington wrote (or it evolved) a dynamic piece in 1928 called *Hot and Bothered*, a wild work, like an angry bee banging about in a jam jar. Constant Lambert, the thirties 'classical' composer, wrote a book called *Music Ho*. In it he praises this piece for its fine musical 'classical' virtues. It had been given the imprimatur of Quality Music by association with the 'classic' field.

That made it OK by us.

I still have a collection of 78rpm olde timers on shellac – jazz records: Vocalian, Columbia, Brunswick, Capitol, Parlophone, Vogue, Decca, Melodisc – stemming from the forties: these comprised the beginning of my jazz collection. I haven't played any of these old shellac recordings for thirty years and the whole collection is packed in two cardboard boxes each displaying the legend 'BAKED BEANS'.

In fact, some of these discs still belong to Keith, who has never had the temerity to ask for them back. I am willing to give them back, but Keith has probably forgotten that I have them. I hope he's not reading this. I always avoid the subject of old jazz on shellac records when I see him. He never says anything.

Anyway, en passant, don't you find it cumbersome to set up an old, dusty gramophone, decide if 78, 45 or 33 speed is required and which record is appropriate, and then find that one or two have *snapped* – the best-loved ones?

I go for the stars

I continued to act as an amateur with 'The Northampton Players' and later at 'The Masque'. Miss Boyle, my art teacher, suggested it was not good to divide one's attention, but I wilfully continued to perform, though I saw the truth of her premise.

Showman Carol ('Mr Discovery') Levis had come to town, visiting our New Theatre, which had been host to a variegated fare from the sublime to the smutty. I had seen the following plays: *The Lady's Not For Burning* with Richard Burton; *The Merchant of Venice* with Donald Wolfit; *Rosmersholm* with Esme Percy; then Basil Sydney, Diana Wynyard and the young John Gielgud – amongst others.

Soon after the war we sat through *Soldiers in Skirts*, an excruciating Civvy

Street whoopee, Felix Mendelssohn and his Hawaiian Serenaders, Ivy Benson and her all-ladies' band, lots of variety shows, magic conjuring, hypnotism acts and vulgar pantos not fit for children. Comedians included Issy Bon, Nosmo King, Gert and Daisy, The Crazy Gang and ITMA.

Carol Levis, a large, puffy, mild Canadian gentleman, toured the land, achieving national fame, even notoriety, with his roller-coaster amateur theatrical talent show. Budding seekers of stardom would audition before the holy man. The publicity spoke of 'HOW YOU CAN BE DISCOVERED!'

Back in the life class, the students asked why I didn't have a go and promised they'd come and cheer me on, so I called at the 'New' and got an audition immediately, such was my charisma.

Inspired by the lure of a glamorous future, I auditioned with my song 'Stompin' at the Graveyard Ball'. Mr Levis didn't appear interested or even to be listening, but, halfway through, he shouted, 'OK! Cut it!' I knew then that I was out.

'Thank you, Mr Adams, for coming,' said Mr Levis. 'You're on! This Friday. See my secretary for times and details, etc. Good luck and may the Lord have mercy on you.' Alleluja!

'Crikey,' I thought.

As I left the theatre I thought this was a smart way of making a few bucks. After all, no performers were paid.

The day came – there didn't seem to be any students present but my Auntie Grace and my father had turned up with the next-door neighbour. There was an infantile gaggle of would-be performers skulking in the wings – and some very noisy young chicks as well. I was wearing what I thought were the smartest clothes I possessed – my serviceable brown Grammar School elbow-padded, threadbare, rather crumpled suit, but with yellow socks, which I thought might beef it up visually. In my nervous state I forgot to remove my bicycle clips. This was remarked upon and I was told to wait in the wings and, when Mr Levis announced me, to jump to it and walk on to the stage, perform my song and exit to any applause that might accrue. If there were no applause, I should exit stage right, quickly, as Mr Levis had informed us that he wasn't insured against riot.

As I hovered in the wings I became conscious of a low prayer-like chanting coming from the stage area, which seemed to be in Tibetan mode. Was I hearing aright? I peeped round the corner of the flat to see what was going on. The stage manager angrily pulled me back. Mr Levis was praying: the audience was preternaturally quiet.

A rambling text was under way, '…and the earth opened her mouth and swallowed them up together with korah when that company died which time the fire devoured two hundred and fifty men and they became a sign – the family of the Haggites of Shun's the family of Ozni the family En the Erites of Arod the children of … Jehosophat…'

I had heard the gossip that followed Mr Levis – that he was touched by 'religious mania', which could surface at any time. I was witnessing the delivery of a holy, hyper inter-mystical message to the audience there and then. Suddenly there was a change of tack:

'…an' now,' snapped Mr Levis, as if in another unusual tongue, 'I'd liketa introdoose to ya to singa ah liddle song fur uz at th' pianer-fordy an', shoor, you're gonna lurve this guy coz maybe a star is in th' makin tonite – yeah – ladies 'n' gennlemen – ah – ah – hold on – I'll be wizyer in a minute – an' here t'play pianner – yep! – John Adam and give him a big 'and … an' here he comes! Wow!'

I walked out on 'the boards', consumed with stage fright and blindly bumped into Levis as he was quickly trying to clear the stage of some wires and rearrange the microphones by the piano whence I was heading. We began to get inextricably entangled, like that classical Greek statue of a naked father and his two naked sons (in my case one) wound round by snakes.

Hysteria was rising. The audience were restless. I thought I heard the hoot of one or two students. By now I had arrived at the piano.

Because the height of the revolving piano stool was much too high, I started to try and wind it down to suit the level of my posterior. It stuck. Panicking as I tried to wrench it loose, my elbow slipped on to the keyboard with a crash, uncannily like the opening chord of Grieg's Piano Concerto.

Mr Levis was making for the wings, dragging some cable that had caught in a hole in the floor cloth, and he was on his knees wrestling with this problem and ignoring me. I thought I saw sparks.

I felt naked. I thought I'd better get on and get out or go under, so I stamped my foot down on the loud pedal, which was like the echoes of a swimming pool. I began to boogie, dried in the second verse and jived my way out of this unhappy scene. The audience increasingly uttered derisory cat-calls.

Perhaps Miss Boyle was right.

I reflected afterwards that I was not quite ready for Stardom.

My Auntie Grace thought I was good.

'Owls'

6
The Wicked City

When one of our more moralistic teachers, Mr Lionel Brooks, heard that I was going to study in London, he warned me, in all good faith, of the dangers of 'The Wicked City' – the lurking rot of its tottering caries, the false baubles of Harrods Emporium, the obscene outpourings of Babel, a veritable Vanity Fair – the city that Miss Holding had earlier warned us of as we shivered in our desks... 'And they shall call his name Bee L. Zeeboobb and all his cities shall be called Abominabobelable.'

Where was I? Ha!

Huzaah! To London! The Wicked City!

Pack up your colours in your old kitbag and smile, smile, smile. Heave yourself up and out of the seductive slough of provincialism and take to the high road that leads to the Wonderful World of Bohemia.

And Chelsea School of Art.

I had failed the intermediate exam and would take it again next year (DV). I didn't want to study for it once more in Northampton.

I had complained about the out-of-date teaching there and the Principal had replied: 'Adams – you can learn something from even the bloodiest fool.'

Maybe he was right. Recently I looked at some of my old work and saw my returned exam pieces, which had been hidden away for years in a cupboard at the Art School, and they are *lousy*.

Yes, I was determined to go to Chelsea; it had a reputation that went before it.

I took my work and showed it to Mr Williamson, the Principal and the father of an actor, Paul, whom I would know in years to come. Although Williamson found my prevailing colour – slate blue – rather drear, as he always found Northampton students' work, he took me on. In the same office at that moment was Vivian Pitchforth, stone deaf because of the Great War, an excellent draughtsman of the old school, who delivered a 'crit' on my work there and then. Needless to say there was no come-back from me to him.

I asked to be excused for a day or two whilst I looked for digs. To go round knocking from door to door asking for a room to sleep in was usually a hopeless, leather-crunching crawl. After the war there was a housing shortage, but I was immediately lucky.

I knocked on a door in Hereford Road, Paddington, in the pouring rain. A kindly looking lady in her fifties put out her head from the basement. On my enquiry she said she had no rooms and retreated behind the door. I clambered wearily up and away. Suddenly she opened the door again and called me inside. I have an honest face.

After giving her a brief resumé of my reasons for being there, her defences crumbled and she granted me the use of a key. I was so relieved that, nervously, I offered her a biscuit from a packet I was carrying. She politely refused.

I had, though, tugged a tender heartstring. Mrs Ibbison, for that was her name (she was a Cypriot), said, when first seeing me, that she thought I looked very sad, like a drowned Norwegian sailor. I was wearing a black duffle coat and there was a hailstorm outside.

We discussed the tariff; I had thirty bob a week to spend on digs with only a little bit more to live on. Outside it began to thunder.

From then on I was to come and go for four months, partly living in her dreadful basement or going back to Northampton to recover when I was not at Chelsea.

For some students, including myself, there is a romance about scruffy, down-at-heel digs (now that I don't have to live in them) – the cheap rent, the ramshackle ambience, even the lingering smell of cabbage, Ascots that explode in the night, grey armour-plated gas meters that seem to have rusted whilst waiting for the man to come, shared lavatories that required a long haul to the top of the house in the middle of the night, holding on – I've known a few lodging houses in my time since then. But this one took the biscuit.

I settled into the Chelsea Art School life – to a point.

I was uneasy to begin with during the first three months. I used to creep away after school to eat a bun and take tea in a cake shop, to which nobody came because it was slightly off the beaten track, before bicycling home or staying for evening life class.

The teaching at Chelsea was of a liberal nature. Students tended to go their own way and others drew energy from their tutors. There were, all told, a score of them in the different departments that were housed in a decrepit ex-chemical laboratory, which, nevertheless, had a ramshackle bespattered charm. These tutors ranged in their approach from Robert Medley, a fine, sensitive painter who was nevertheless 'economical with the attendance', to Raymond Coxon, a punchy North Country man who slapped the paint on and called a paint brush a paint brush. He was the life class teacher in charge of nudes and we took part in art-orientated quizzes while the model rested.

In between were the Red Terror and Marxist scribe, John Berger, and the intelligent, self-effacing Prunella Clough (I studied 'Still Life' with her) who, by the time she was 80, had realised a certain profundity.

Julian Trevelyan started off as a surrealist at the time of the 1936 exhibition, but later developed a rather over-pretty style.

My favourite art teacher was Ceri Richards – an exciting, eclectic quasi-surrealist who found his inspirational sources in Dylan Thomas's poetry, Debussy, costerwomen, 'Woman Playing the Piano', and who transformed Trafalgar Square into a colourful bazaar à la Matisse. Max Ernst's gloom of old, which had formerly been one inspiration, had disappeared.

The HM, Mr Williamson, was a cadaverous éminence grise – more grise than éminence – and his sidekick, Fred Brill, was physically opposed to Williamson and a jolly, rumbustious character.

At school I used to admire the noble-looking Elisabeth Frink as she passed me in the corridor. Everyone seemed so sophisticated I felt a bit out of it. It might have been a young ladies' finishing school. The accents were glassy. There existed the whole phonetic world of upper-class labial consonants and dipthongs to fascinate the ears, and a new Passing Parade to watch – the children of colonels – old Etonians – the progeny of wealthy bankers – belted earls – unbelted earls … and the daughter of the Ambassador to Costa Rica (whom I was to know so well).

'The Stunt'

Every Christmas the Art School put on a maverick performance called 'The Stunt'. It was a kind of sophisticated panto, or un-intimate revue, written by the students. In the finale all the teachers appeared en masse, some looking distinctly embarrassed, to sing some relevant number, and those with histrionic talent could perform a sketch or event. Old pupils and teachers would turn up out of loyalty and to renew old acquaintances.

Back home in Northampton, before arriving in London, I used to 'tinkle' with the pianoforte in the drawing-room and, with my growing interest in jazz, I gave birth to some cabaret-style songs in the jazz idiom. I thought I'd try them out in 'The Stunt' on this my first Christmas at the Art School. I was amazed at their reception. The audience 'went mad'. I boogied.

And they clamoured for encores.

My life at Chelsea suddenly changed from that moment.

I become a Minor Cult

From now on I was fêted at parties as a highbrow troubadour of sorts and enjoyed a sudden entrée to the Chelsea Arty Set. I was, in fact, a minor clownish cult.

One night, at a party, I was advised that a music agent was prowling around and that, for my own good, I must quickly sing before he disappeared. Of course, this made me more nervous than usual. However, the deed was done, the pianoforte was duly hammered to:

> 'Stompin' at the Graveyard Ball'
> 'It Happened in the Chapel in the Valley'
> 'I'm a Tipsy Dipsomaniac'
> 'Rockin' with Little Mo Muffet'
> 'The Beelzebub Boogie'

The agent turned out to be one Jim Godbolt, who was then managing Mick Mulligan's Magnolia Jazz Band with George Melly as chanteur. Jim was building up a reputation as an entrepreneur in trad jazz circles.

A man of trenchant and pithy humour, he was 'as straight as a die' in an environment that was sometimes of doubtful probity. He was usually conventionally dressed, often wearing a mackintosh over his sleek, live-wired body, and his face was amusingly vulpine. He had a charming girlfriend who was beginning to tire of following the workaholic Jim to some dreadful venue every night looking for talent.

He introduced himself and agreed to 'try me out'.

I remember singing (shouting, according to Jim Godbolt) in a dark cellar à la 'left bank' called Le Club du Faubourg.

An appearance at the Nuffield Centre in Trafalgar Square did me no favours. I failed to appreciate that this venue was the haunt of the Gordon Highlanders let out and off the leash for the evening. I was howled off the stage.

Why does one do it (as they say)?

The Studio Club in Piccadilly was a more restful rendezvous. Amidst the motley, sometimes mottled, cider imbibers were two definitely non arty-farty figures – Hamish Moffat and John Drummond.

They were both vintage automobile freaks, well-spoken and mannerly but falling down on their haute couture. Hamish always wore torn khaki shorts covered in oil. He drove a 1924 Lagonda, which was his obsession. John Drummond drove an equally antique automobile. He and Hamish were the descendants, but prettier, of the archetypal Mr Toad.

Drummond was less oily than Hamish, but had a habit of wobbling his very elegant head to and fro whilst driving due to some cranial disturbance of the abdullah oblong garter. He was the Stirling Moss of surfing, swerving and surviving. For all we know he is still at large and loose upon the roads of this very borough.

My oily friends were a disturbing sight to the managers of night clubs who wanted to maintain a smart image.

One night Hamish, covered in oil as he'd just finished mending a motorbike outside in Piccadilly Circus, led a slouch of students – Lis, Arthur, Ann, Blom, Peter, Drummond and others – into gatecrashing this louche club to hear me sing my songs.

The manager wasn't amused:

(1) They hadn't booked
(2) They didn't buy many drinks
(3) Two of the patrons were covered in oil

Luckily for me the in-crowd was vociferous in their favourable response.

Kings Road and its denizens

After the war, the prevailing philosophical zeitgeist was Existentialism, with a dollop of angst thrown in by Jean-Paul Sartre. It was thought to be the cult of negativism and utter despair – indeed, cosmic blues. In short, look after yourself because no one else will and God's gone to bed. Thus the 'colour' black became the flag of these emotions and Paris the centre of this sombre haute couture.

Female students soon began wearing black, skin-tight, figure-hugging costumes with floppy tops. My duffle coat was black and I went out and about, almost bald, with the 'new crew cut'. Girls' make-up was severe – the face a ghostly white against black ringed eyes and shiny, white gloss lips…

The Kings Road was the nearest you could get to Paris's la rive gauche – a tatterdemalion tottering fabric of ateliers, garrets, creaking, ivy-overgrown studios, with the glass beginning to craze – they had housed a plethora of creative people who had lived and worked in Chelsea and still did:

Augustus John, Lyn Chadwick, Laurie Lee, Theodore Garman, Elisabeth Frink, Bernard Meadows, Willy Soukop, Prunella Clough, Ceri Richards, Oscar Wilde, Peter Warlock, Reg Butler, Robert Medley, Rupert Doone, Raymond Coxon, John Minton, Rodrigo Moynihan, Louis MacNeice, Robert Buhler, Peter Ustinov, Henry Moore, Graham Sutherland, Roger Hilton, Terry Frost, William Scott, Stephen Gardiner, Julian Bream, Mary Quant…

Now, being in Chelsea, it behoved me to establish myself in a central drab, suitably scruffy 'atelier' befitting an apprentice of Bohemia's beckoning woods and fields (in a manner of speaking).

I moved.

It was a perfect situation. My new decrepit bedsit was now at the top of No 272 Kings Road – an eighteenth-century terraced house that is now the fire station. It couldn't have been better. It was on the corner of Manresa Road, two minutes walk from the Art School. Over the road, just visible from my window, was Hemmings, the old-fashioned cake shop and café, well used at break time by the students. The young David Sylvester, lugubrious art guru and now an authority on Francis Bacon, would walk past, stop, retreat, peer at the cakes, remain fixed as if in meditation, then disappear into the shop to make a purchase from the patisserie. I was opposite Peter Ustinov's house – a large, well-favoured eighteenth-century building. I would see him shuffle out and scan his letters at the open front door.

In between was Oakley Street, where lived Elisabeth Frink and Arthur, the delightful Shirley Blomfield, known as Blom, her friend Peter Hawkins, and Ann Irving, with whom I would be spending more and more time.

Ann

I became part of the arty mob by a process of osmosis. We all tended to live in Oakley Street on or off or thereabouts.

As a chansonnier I was soon invited from my pad in Kings Road over to Oakley Street for a party given by Ann Irving, the delightful Shirley Blomfield (Ann's friend Blom), Lis Frink and Arthur, who all lived in the same house.

Ann Irving was a daughter of the Ambassador to Costa Rica. Well brought up, she was a charming girl, small and jolly, filled with plenty of gigglement and with a rather moral attitude to life – religious even. Her paintings were seen as through a glass darkly. She suited my puritanism. She was a painter. Like sails on a ship, quite large canvasses appeared to engulf her when she tried to move them around the room for a new vantage point.

She had a weakness for rough cider, as I soon did, at fivepence halfpenny a glass, at the Six Bells.

Of course, I cannot remember, some fifty years later, the minutiae of this event, but a lot of students were lolling on the floor, loud with exuberance. Cider and beer flowed through the veins in a Bacchic torrent – was that the moon I could see through the window? Two chaste moons?

'Moon up above – everyone in love…'

'Boop a doop.'

I became aware that I was lying against Ann, holding her hand. She had not taken her hand away from mine, nor had I taken my hand away from hers. The pleasure was profound. I was moved by the mystery of it. How could such a minimal touching of the body issue forth such profound feelings of delight? I sank into a static state of reverie that seemed to last for ever…

Two moons had long melted – orange light percolated through the curtains – the hectic shrieks of the night had given way to snoring and whispering – bodies slumped against furniture or each other. Now people were beginning to stumble off silently, as in a dream, into the dawn. In London the first red bus is the herald of the day.

Ann and I had dozed off. She woke me. There was a long silence.

'Would you like to go for a walk?' she said.

I can't remember what we said as we walked together beside the Embankment. I can only remember a feeling of well-being.

We returned. Back at the door of No 93, she made some apology and asked, 'Would you like to come to tea later this afternoon, John?'

I stuttered, 'Yes, please.'

It wasn't much longer before we kissed. She was to lead me into Bohemian paths – a jolly, if brief, life with the set.

Ann and I would often go to the 'flicks' to see the latest cultural French classic – at the Classic Cinema, *Orphée*, Jacques Tati, *Le Diable au Corps*, *Bicycle Thieves*, Buñuel – a forbidden showing of *Un Chien Andalou* and *L'age D'or* – of surrealist ilk.

There lived at No 272 Kings Road Theodore Garman, son of Epstein's liaison with the formidable Kathleen Garman, oft-time model who was to become Lady Epstein. He was a monumental figure, seemingly always ensconced in a long, thick, dark, threadbare coat, somewhat bestrewn with paint, certainly à la bohême, who spoke with the Lower East Side of his father's New York background, mixed with a gruff English.

Extremely over-sensitive, be was well-loved by those who knew him and I got to know of the naiveté that masks profundity. He painted on a large scale – a tour de force of expressionism – writhing vegetation and buildings created from layers of rich impasto.

Scattered around his crumbling sitting-room were ethnic sculptures, or small works by his father.

The studio, a ramshackle shed at the bottom of a garden, suffered attacks from flooding. In winter, to get from A to B, one had to tread water, preferably having previously pulled on galoshes in order to splosh one's way to advancement.

Theodore was given to instability and had spent some time in St Andrew's Hospital, Northampton, an establishment that seems to haunt these pages, the clientele often being drawn from the famous.

Theo wasn't popular with my new landlady. He complained one day that she had thrown a bucket of water over him whilst leaning from the second-floor window. He was merely wishing to pay me a visit. Maybe his eccentricity disturbed some people, but this was gross behaviour towards a gentle soul. My landlady wondered why I was so angry with her.

Theo died brutally. He was apprehended taking one of the classical plaster casts from the School of Art sculpture studio to his nearby room, just over Manresa Road, presumably to borrow and study it in all innocence. The School Authorities sent for the police and an ambulance. In a struggle with male nurses he suffered a fatal heart attack.

He was aged twenty-nine.

'Preening queen'

Up, and perambulating down, the Kings Road was a sight for sore arses – the flamboyant Quentin Crisp was on mince-about. Supermodel, artist and artiste, writer and over-the-tiptop raconteur – 'One of the Stately Homos of England' (to repeat Mr Crisp's own 'Cowardy' picturesque description) – he was a raffish gentleman who flaunted his sexual proclivities and wit in the firing line of the hoi-polloi who, sneering with mockery and menace, would beat him for his pains.

A lust for attention led him to re-invent himself to camp up his haute couture to an ithyphallic extravaganza – often wearing a velvet suit. On a chilly day he would don a mantle with fur-lined pelisse, topped by a fedora (one more elegant in its shaping and curvatures than is usual in such headwear). Round the neck was draped a silken cravat with frilly jabot at the base, completed by crepe-soled Hush Puppy brothel-creepers. The face whitened with foundation and summarily rouged about the cheeks, eyelids and lashes shadowed with kohl and mascara, hair hennaed and lacquered.

The whole construct was brought to a halt – en garde! – by a dramatic coup de théâtre – cerise lip gloss.

And all this long before the days of *The Rocky Horror Show*.

This daily ritual was created in humble circumstances – a shabby bedsit that never felt the flick of a duster or maybe even light of day.

He was a truly professional artists' model and a master of pose and poise, prepared to proffer himself at the request of the moment. Having attended several Art School Life Classes in my time, I regret that I never saw him standing on his head for half an hour, an extraordinary posture which was reputed to be a veritable tour de force to those who drew it.

More's the pity that the discipline of life drawing has long withered and models such as Mr Crisp are scarce seen on the dais these days. I did, though, occasionally pass him on the Kings Road and give him a wink.

The Wicked City again

'Hullo, Mr Brooks!'

He jumped. I whispered darkly.

'And its name shall be called BeeeeelZeeBUB.'

'I beg your pardon.'

'And your works will be called ABOMINABLEAABOL.BOL.'

I was walking along Kings Road, Chelsea, minding my own business under an orange-coloured sky some time in the future and happy as a sandbag, when who should I career into but my erstwhile gloomy Northamptonian pedagogue, Mr Lionel Brooks.

He asked me how I was getting on at Chelsea and I said that I was enjoying myself. I told him I was even performing cabaret in the dark caverns of Soho and…

Brooks hastily stopped me with a warning, signalled by a hectic spot in his cheeks, exclaiming, 'The Wicked City! Oh! I told you to beware – not to lurk in the nightly pursuit of Modernismus in the dens of Mandrax and Jazz or follow Picasso's ass – you should be concentrating on nude drawing: form, form and again, *form*! The watchword is, follow Disgustus John – he is the master of Form today,' and with a hollow laugh off he strutted to deliver his picture for the RA Summer Exhibition, but hung it on the railings of the Bayswater Road instead.

I shouted after him, 'I will dance one day on the tomb of your Sir Alfred Munnings. May the Academy burn!'

Then I awoke and behold it was all a dream…

Would you like to meet Van Gogh?

I was traipsing around the Cork Street area – Cork Street of artistic fame – with a portfolio of my work to show to any gallery that might be prepared to grant me an audience.

I entered one gallery, introduced myself and invited the director to sample my wares. He retorted that his gallery didn't look at new work – they had got enough on their books already.

I suggested to him that he might be rejecting a masterpiece and, who knows, I could be another Van Gogh.

He replied, 'If you were another Van Gogh, I think we'd have heard of you by now. Good day.'

A rest among the test-tubes

Running alongside the Chelsea Library and my new Temple of Art was a chemistry laboratory manned by pharmaceutical boffins in long white coats. Once in those early days, mistaking it for the public library, I entered this laboratory in order to borrow a book about Rosa Bonheur, only to be forced into retreat by odoriferously foul fumes that released in me a fit of graveyard retching. Some slight allergy perhaps?

This was a rude re-awakening to the pungency of chemicals. As a boy I enjoyed playing with my toy chemistry set – now the smells seduced me again. Methylated spirits – camphor – cobalt chloride – iodine – flowers of sulphur, etc. A hint of the schoolish stinks from the sulphurated hydrogen apparatus being mischievously turned on surrounding the slumped figure of Sleepy Nelson dozing amidst the soporific fumes – a remembrance of smells past.

Frink

As soon as I saw Elisabeth Frink's work, I knew that she was destined for recognition as a major British artist. We wondered how one so young could create such mature and authoritative work. The present of the artist 'at work' in the vicinity was a great stimulus – fierce, angular drawings wrought in black ink on large sheets of virgin newsprint – sinister birds of doubtful lineage – black crows exposing shards of bare brittle bones – an amazingly varied bestiary, dominated by the horse – plaster-hewn images of brutish, gold-eyed, goggled men – images that continued to dominate her work throughout her career – the secular to the religious.

Two men with a hang glider

The suffering Christ bound at the pillar

Fallen man...

It was at this time of angst after the war – atom bombs – the Cold War – the images of concentration camps – 'The Beast of Belsen' – that the all-purpose intellectual éminence grise, Herbert Read, coined the concept 'The Geometry of Fear', applying it to artists like Chadwick, Richier, Armitage and Butler – winner of the 'Unknown Political Prisoner' prize. (My father gave this latter a verbal basting when he spotted it reproduced in the *Daily Express*.)

These artists were recognisable by their international geometric semi-abstract style.

Frink was as sensitive, as were any of these artists, if not more so, to the horror of war – she had been in the firing and bombing lanes in Kent as a girl, but she played no part in these artists' aesthetic arena. There was no hint of their geometric style in her work, but an expressionist figuration which, to my mind, was far more redolent of fear than the platitudes and clichés of the 'Geometry of Fear' school.

I had the privilege of working, literally, by her side in the sculpture studio – the teachers were Willi Soukop and Bernard Meadows – on a Friday afternoon, with few other students working, as, on Fridays, they tended to dribble off home early. It was suggested that, although I was 'studying painting', I should make the most of a free Friday place and try my hand at sculpture.

Lis was usually bejeaned or trousered in black, her firm figure striding along the corridor bespattered with plaster. By the end of the day some had reached her hair, which was now chalky-white and fluffed as she disappeared in a cloud of powder into the sculpture room, starting slowly to roll a fag whilst staring at her work in progress, assessing her next sculptural stratagem.

Physically she was extraordinarily like her own created images. Was she created by Nature in its own image? Or did her own image create Nature?

She looked – well – Roman – a certain masculine quality, lissom but tough, strongly female – her love was always for a 'he-man' or 'red-blooded male.' Her hands were those of a sculptor, fortuitously large and made for pummelling the clay or hacking at the plaster. Her nose – aquiline – her blue eyes warm towards one at times.

She was shy.

She was pulled in (by me when I could twist her arm) to join or direct bits of 'The Stunt' – she wasn't too happy and felt embarrassed, but thought she ought to do her bit. Recently I drew out of my nostalgia cupboard 'The Stunt' programme for 1952, and noted that Lis performed on stage a ditty called 'A Girl With An Urge'. I cannot say I remember it, but, knowing her shyness, it was brave of her.

Another surprise is the knowledge that she posed nude at the Royal College and St Martin's life classes. This doesn't tally with her reticence. She was no Quentin Crisp, the doyen of models around this time.

Lis's living room at No 93 Oakley Street was cluttered with her sculptures. One day, my elbow was feeling tired and I placed it clumsily on the mantelshelf, knocking over one of her evil-looking plaster birds, which fell into the grate, broken. I was horror-struck.

'Don't worry,' said Lis, who was standing by. 'Have it!'

She said this without a hint of rancour or displeasure.

I thanked her for her magnanimity.

I picked up the bits and took them away.

Life continued.

Later, I tried to mend it.

I held on to it. Years later it collapsed and was no more.

Lis was living with Arthur Collings, a generous enough man, subject to mood swings. He had been a Pathfinder for Bomber Command during the war and was shot down, injured and taken prisoner. This had unbalanced him and he would go on benders, disappearing into the welter of Chelsea stews, heavy with drink and tortured by anxiety. The bush telegraph would send signals and Lis, Ann, Blom, Peter, Arthur's sister, myself and any one who was around would go hunting in all the pubs seeking his whereabouts. They would be searches fraught with tension – Arthur had undergone a leucotomy and took paraldehyde to stabilise his condition. The odour could be quite strong and was thus a warning signal. There was the ever-present threat of suicide to add another dimension to the search. From amiability he could veer and teeter on the brink of dangerous anger.

Once we were all invited to a full-dress military knees-up at the Chelsea Barracks. We were in scruffy student wear. One officer began to question us and asked to see our invitation cards, which we had lost. He suggested that we leave. Things began to get nasty before Arthur rose to the occasion. Lis moved in with smooth talk and tried to pacify Arthur who was becoming more and more menacing. When we happened to mention the name of the officer who had given us the entrée, the said officer began to bend over backwards, and forwards, mumbling humbling apologies. Gently Lis began to steer Arthur away.

A narrow escape.

Lis could be protective and cosseting to men like Arthur, damaged in the war, as she was to the men who followed. She instinctively sensed that under their powerful male frames, they too were vulnerable. They looked like her sculptures.

Eventually Arthur took an overdose.

Shy during the day and cool, Lis's evenings and nights were wild with drink, jive and jollity, but the next day she was up and about in the studio on time at ten o'clock prompt.

She was shy.
She was protective.
She was wild.

Spots: was my face red?

During my adolescence I had been attacked by galloping acne (propionibacterium) and attended therapy at Northampton General, where my face was subjected to blasting by electric rays that roasted my epidermis and left my spots hubble-bubbling as if retrieved straight from a microwave.

After treatment I would turn up at the Northampton Art School to join the life class, carrying a bright red face (was my face red?), my physiognomy as sore as a monkey's posterior.

'Here comes Chapel,' might come the cry, so called because of my miserable-looking mien.

The disease continued into my time at Chelsea, when I changed my general practitioner to a Dr Rachel Pinney, in her forties, a small and portly doctor of Freudian psychiatry with some reputation in the arty confines of Chelsea. She owned No 93 Oakley Street and one would often pass the slightly open door of her room and observe her lying exhausted on the sofa after a hard day's skull-duggery. I was recommended by the Oakley Street crowd to ask her to advise me on the subject of my pustules. Knowing something of my chaste relationship with Ann, she diagnosed that the facial eruptions were the symptoms of sexual repression and that I was suffering from Virginity. She therefore advised a course of Onanism. I suggested that this might be bad for the eyesight, but she said that this canard was an 'old optician's tale' with religious connotations but, nevertheless, better safe than sorry – make it a rule; Never on Sundays.

'Oh, blow!'

The months rubbed by and this dicky problem seemed to clear up naturally. The last time I saw Dr Pinney was in Trafalgar Square at a CND rally where she was haranguing an audience on the threat of nuclear war. She had long refused to speak every Wednesday as long as Britain retained the atom bomb. She would button her lips on that day, in protest.

I meet Melly

We, the Chelsea lot, used to attend the Royal College of Art dances, which grew more and more degenerate – at least for a country boy – although not as degenerate as the famous Chelsea Arts Ball, which was eventually closed down because of incipient chaos and a burgeoning sexual whathaveyou.

Back at the Royal College dance, I vaguely remember helping the charismatic and etiolated John Minton remove sickened revellers from the lavatories, placing them in rows outside for air … to the savage sound of Mick Mulligan's Jazz Band fronted by the young George Melly. He was not the gentle, obese gangster we knew later, with no big-brimmed hat and coat of loud check, but presented a persona on stage that was a cross between the late Bessie Smith and a surrealist jazz Antichrist, strutting to the beat, his fingers forming an inverted cross as he shimmied and blasphemed his stuff to the sweating dancers. He would lunge down and kiss in abandon any girls that found themselves in the firing line up front.

His voice was very resonant in those days and he presented a seductive image.

The high point of the evening was his performance of 'Frankie and Johnny', an illusionistic cabaret turn where, with his back to the audience, two separate floating hands would creepily appear, hugging his hips and erotically massaging his writhing body. Today he has more fat on him – rather like King Ubu. I would advise him, before it's too late, that it's not a sin to take off your skin and dance around in your bones.

It was a little later that my music agent, Jim Godbolt, invited me to meet Melly at his flat, knowing that as an eclectic surrealist myself and an enthusiastic Jazz Fiend, I would like to meet what one might term 'the Genuine Article'. When I arrived at Jim's flat, Melly was already there with a silent young girl decorating the sofa.

Tongues loosened and I heard all about that obscene painting 'Le Viol' by Magritte – a painting with a radical relocation of body parts that has a most disturbing effect – not the only artist to do this. The surrealists were often driven to dislocate form – from the melting watches of Dali to the extreme dismemberment employed by Picasso (which came first – Picasso or Surrealism?) – a Klee he had just bought – the polar opposite to Magritte.

Whilst all this was being sieved through the head – crack snap shellac of the 78 – Louis Armstrong was singing scat – do bah doo boo – 'Pure Dada!'

cried Melly, delighted. 'Advert in the underground – grapes oozing out of a grape crusher – a Freudian symbol – New Orleans now – Mr Jelly Lord – Sidney Bechet – too sweet with his vibrato – my sister caught me in the solitary act of what Stendhal called…?'

George now found himself shifting nearer and nearer to the young girl who had been sitting on the sofa not saying a word. In spite of George's growing attention to her, she remained as immobile as an Easter Island statue. Inflamed and now grumpy with rebuff, George threw himself on the floor, grousing about the puritanism of the young folk these days.

The evening broke up of its own volition – the girl disappeared. George lunged at me and I said I'd go too. Outside in the night I was quickly unlocking my bicycle when George's head appeared round the corner and invited me to come up to see his Paul Klee's some time. George was beginning to steam. I fled with just enough air in my tyres to get me round the block. (I was only a country boy!)

I had first met George Melly at the surrealist London gallery. He was then acting as a factotum for Eduard Mesens. The gallery was financed soon after the war by E. L. T. Mesens, who dressed like a businessman (indeed, was one) and was a creator of small delicate collages, as well as being a poet.

Melly had left the Navy, with its rum bum and sodomy, and, fascinated by what he had seen of surrealism in books and legend, found his way to its temple in the 'Barcelona Restaurant' in Beak Street, Soho, a shabby den where anarchists lurked among pacifists, socialists and various subversives.

Soon E.L.T. signed Melly up to help in the shop and he began to gain a knowledge of surrealist business. He was in this mode when I met him and E. L. T. Mesens – me, a young lad of sixteen, then rather apprehensive.

I was with my Art School on a trip from Northampton to some exhibition or other and had planned to break loose from the party and discover Surrealism's base in London's Brook Street.

I arrived there, having shaken off the gang, and found myself facing the window: it displayed a 'Portrait of Valentine' by Max Ernst – in blue – all right so far – with a suggestion of his alter ego, 'Lop Lop Superior of the Birds' in the corner.

I entered the shrine throbbing with excitement. Four baleful eyes focused on my gauche gait and nervous youth as I crept in, pretending they weren't there and stumbling on to view the exhibition, which was of Magritte's work – that most despised of artists then. Indeed, was he an artist? Clive Bell would not have seen much 'Significant Form' in him.

The baleful eyes still watched me. Unable to stand the tension, I whipped round.

Me: Er … hi. (*A pause*)

E.L.T.: Bonjour, M'sieur.

Me: Are you a surrealist by nature? (*A pause*)

E.L.T.: Am I a surrealist by nature? (*He turns to Melly*) Is André Breton a surrealist by nature? Ha!

E.L.T. slowly waddled across the thick, pile carpeting towards a little bookshelf and six postcards and drew down what I now know was Nadeau's *History of Surrealism* and, opening a page, displayed photos of all the surrealists. Pointing his stubby finger, he located the relevant photo. (*A pause*) Nothing more was to be said. After another whip round the Magrittes, I asked whether there were any surrealist books for sale. George gravely told me (he had a different persona as bookseller) that they had a copy of Ernst's 'collage novel' *Une Semaine de Bonte*, but when I heard the price I must have appeared shaken and declined the offer. I then turned my attention to a surrealist pamphlet and asked the price of that.

'One shilling,' said E.L.T. (*A pause*) And now it seemed that he was working out some obtuse numismatic problem…

'…but as the boy appears to be interested in Surrealism … sixpence.'

I bought it there and then. I have it now, rotting in my library on the shelves of my Surrealist section. It is headed 'Idolatry and Confusion'.

It was written by E.L.T.

The last time I saw Melly was at a theatre in Barnet where he ruminated on his life in front of a polite audience. At question time, a woman increasingly began to make herself known, gibbering to him in arcane gobbledegook and gradually creeping towards him until she arrived on all fours at his knee. The audience began to wonder what this was – a surrealist 'happening' perhaps?

The woman pulled up his trouser leg and observed the exposed leg. After a minute's silence, George spoke uttering the one word, 'Psoriasis.'

Spain

Towards the end of my Chelsea life Hamish took me as a passenger with Daphne, his girlfriend, and Peter Hawkins all the way through Spain in his Lagonda, from Biarritz to Dos Hermanas near Seville, where I had planned to paint.

It was a wonderful experience apart from the fact that I started off on this journey suffering from quinsy, gastro-enteritis and a touch of depression, which persisted all the way, thus necessitating stopping off at numerous doctors' surgeries and convents where nuns would inject me with new-fangled antibiotics, forcing me into spending more money than I should have. I wonder if leaving Chelsea and Ann might have depressed me.

In 1953, as soon as you crossed the Pyrenees and entered Spain you were in Africa. Deserts and palms, ruined temples, ancient castles, peasants, the sinister Guardia Seville, Chiricoesque architecture, or I think it is Churriguerresque architecture.

In thrall to Hamish's expert driving, we sped on and on and through and through – once through a raised roundabout, which broke the axle.

This was soon mended at a garage where Hamish, inflamed by the mañana mañana lassitude of the mechanics, seized the tools and mended it himself while they watched, fascinated.

The Lagonda was a *sensation*. The further south we drove, the larger the mob that gathered round, just silently staring in the Iberian manner. We would search for a restaurant while the mob followed. Occasionally, we would feel little projectiles aimed at us as we sat at table waiting for our paella. But, in general, the locals would go out of their way to help and were friendly.

This was where Peter discovered that he had no money left, so he turned round and had to hitch-hike back before reaching Seville. We were sad but we had only enough money for our own needs. He lived then on apples taken from orchards.

I was dumped in Dos Hermanas, as agreed, with the heartening thought that I would be picked up by Hamish a fortnight later after I had painted some pictures.

Off they went.

There was no hotel. I found myself living above the grocer's shop. My bed was of prickly straw. I had to pick my way through a roomful of sleeping bodies when it was siesta time. My meals comprised tomatoes, bread and wine. The only other 'amenities' were a water tap and a pot for defecation.

Over the road was a bar in which I gradually grew to know the men during their nightly natters when they practised their fractured English on me. Very laborious.

When my fortnight was over there was no Lagonda. I waited. And waited. The days passed. It got hotter and hotter.

So, packing several packets of cheapo 'Goya' cigarettes and flyblown comestibles, I limped my way back on the hitch-hike trail. I had very, very little money and was spending a few nights in ditches.

I made it to Dieppe and beyond – reaching home.

My father thought I was a brown skeleton.

There had been some mistake.

The gloomy threat of imminent National Service hung over us. Both Ann and I were beginning to admit to this and we were drifting away from each other. Ann regularly kept a diary in a very scrawly handwriting. Once she left it on a desk, open. (For me to read perhaps?) It said, 'John is very amusing but I don't love him.' She began gravitating towards another student and finally sent me a letter saying, 'Darling John, thank you for giving me a year of your life.'

When we parted I found myself at West Kirby in the RAF.

In later years Ann married and had four children. A prey to unhappiness, she eventually took her own life.

7
National Service

Hymn to West Kirby RAF (3141603) –
The party was over

'BADGES BUTTONS BLOUSES BLANCO BRASSO BATTLEDRESS BROMIDE BULL AND BOLLOCKS GETCHA FUCKIN' FEET ON THE FUCKIN' DECK HANDS OFF COCKS AND ON WITH SOCKS YOUR MOTHER WOULDN'T WANNA SEE THAT LADDIE ONE TWO THREE ONE TWO THREE ONE TWO THREE ON THE SPOT NOW LEFT RIGHT LEFT RIGHT LEFT RIGHT LEFT RIGHT MAKE IT SNAPPY OR YOU'LL BE OVER THE WALL. WHAT'S YOUR NAME SONNY BOY?'

'Adams, Corp.'

'ADAM SIR! WOT'S YOUR NUMBER ADAM?'

'3141603.'

'LOUDER.'

'3. 1. 4. 1. 6. 0. 3!'

'WHAT'S THAT?'

'3141603, Corp!'

'WELL ADAM – OR MAY I CALL YOU SUNSHINE? YES SUNSHINE COS I'LL MAKE THE SUN SHINE OUTTA YOUR ARSE ADAM BEFORE I'VE DONE WITH YOU. WHAT SHINES OUTTA YOUR ARSE?'

'The sun shines out of my arse.'

'ARSE?'

'Arse, Corp!'

'ONLY 729 DAYS MORE TO DO LADDIE. 'OW MANY DAYS MORE?'

'73 – 729 days.'

'YOU LOOK LIKE A VULTURE THAT'S SHIT I'SELF YOU … YOU 'ORRIBLE LIDDLE MAN. WHAT ARE YOU?'

'I'm a horrible little man, Corporal, SAH.'

'I'M WATCHIN' YOU – FALL OUT THE FOLLOWIN': JEHOVAH'S WITNESSES, R.C. CAT'LICS, CHRISTIAN SCIENTISTS, HOTTENTOTS. FALL OUT! ONE TWO ONE TWO ONE TWO ONE TWO ONE TWO.'

'ADAM 3141? WHA'S THIS? I THOUGHT I SAID THAT ALL YOUR PERS'NAL KIT SHOULD BE SQUARED UP – WHA'S ALL THIS? WHA'S ALL THIS? SQUARED UP? MY MOTHER MAKES PLUM PUDDINGS A GOOD SIGHT SQUARER THAN THAT – AND SHE MAKES 'EM IN A FUCKIN' ROUND BASIN YOU 'ORRIBLE LIDDLE MAN. WHAT ARE YOU?'

'A 'orrible little man, Corporal.'

'LOOK ATCHER FUCKIN' BOOTS. GET AT THOSE TOE CAPS, ADAM – BURNISH WITH SPOON, SCALD PIMPLES OFF, HEAT UP SPOON, SPIT AND POLISH BRIGHT 'N' SHINY LIKE AN EFFIN MIRROR. TAKE ALL YOUR BLOODY EFFIN EVENIN'. FOGGIN BLOODY HELL! STAND BY YOUR BEDS AND OUTTA YOUR FUCKIN' PIT, JACK. WHA' ARE YOU, ADAM?'

'A 'orrible little man, Corporal.'

'YOU WEREN'T BORN YOU WERE TOSSED OFF AGAIN' A WALL AND THE SUN HATCHED YOU OUT. ONE TWO ONE TWO ONE TWO ONE TWO… DON'T LOOK DOWN, FEEL FOR THE TRIGGER. IF IT HAD 'AIR ROUND IT YOU'D FIND IT MATE. PER ADU ARSE TRA IS OUR MOTTO SO RESPEC' IT YOU SKIVIN' SHITEHAWK ADAM WHA' ARE YOU?'

'A skiving shithouse, Corp.'

'WHAT'S THAT? 3141603?

'Shitehawk, Corp.'

'PACK UP YOUR CIVVIES. PARCEL UP WIV BROWN PAPER AND STRING. KITBAG LINED UP, GROUND SHEET, MESS TINS, IRONS, BOOTS, BLANKETS. BUMPER WHOLE PLACE WITH PADS, GET BROOM HANDLES. RAZOR. SMOOTH SWEEP. GET 'EM SQUARED! WOOLLEN KHAKI SHIRTS, GAITERS, WEBBING, BERET, BOOTS. GET THAT CREASED! SHIRTS, PANTS, *SQUARE IT*, SCRUB, BUMPER, *BULL IT*, SCRUB, SCOUR… AM I 'URTIN' YOU, LADDIE? YOU SHOULD BE 'URTIN' – I'M STANDIN' ON YOUR 'AIR. GET IT *OFF* BY TWELVE HUNDRED HOURS AT THE BLEEDIN' BA BA, LAD! OH YOU 'ORRIBLE LITTLE MAN. WHA' ARE YOU?'

'I'm a horrible little man. Who are you? I mean – what am I? I mean what are you? I mean when will you…?'

After three months of that I was very pleased when it was all over – it knocked me into shape and made a man of me. I've never recovered.

I elected to become a medic. In the camp at Lytham St Annes life was more reasonable than of late and it was interesting to study medicine in a relaxed environment (eg in our icy Nissen hut in winter). My co-medics were interesting characters, a Buddhist, a Conservative planning to be a politician, a budding artist, Kirby Green, who became a friend and who now runs a tiny festival in Brightlingsea, and a ballet-dancer who produced a variety show.

One day we all gathered around a WAAF to hear where we would exercise our 'trade' for the next year and a half – mine was as a medic in *Malaya*! I had not volunteered to go abroad. I planned to spend my time skiving in the same camp, all cosy, in a little hut constructing and painting plaster medical demonstration models that show all the macho muscles and bleeding hearts. There was a job going that I hoped to nobble where you could listen to the Third Programme ad nauseam.

But now – *Malaya* – the images of the magic east swam before me. In 1953 nobody except the ex-pats went to Malaya. There were no holidays on beaches with palm trees. The working classes were still in Jaywick Sands. This was an opportunity to visit Foreign Lands – a part of the crumbling Empire.

Our Sergeant Instructor advised us that the Far East posting was a 'Cook's Tour'. Not to touch the lovely apples – they're rotten. I wasn't to know that I would be visiting the great temple of Angkor Wat.

So, saying goodbye to my friends, I hoisted my kitbag on my back, sang a merry song and climbed up into the aeroplane and began the flight that would take me, in a week, way across the world…

My father, from this time on, was a wonderful correspondent and kept me in touch.

Letters from Malaya

13th April 1954
Changi
Arrived here last night. It is a wonderful camp, in fact almost a small town of flats (which are the billets) which remind one of a Soviet Workers Paradise. There are naffis and clubs open all day and nobody seems to do any work. I see the reason why people refer to Far East postings as a 'Cook's Tour'.

One of the medics and I have been posted to a place with the romantic Malayan name of Butterworth, which is near Georgetown on Penang island and not far from the Siamese/Malay frontier.

We start tomorrow on a two days' train journey through the jungle via Kuala Lumpur and will be issued with rifles, as we might be shot at or the track mined.

18th April 1954
RAF Butterworth
Arrived here yesterday safe and sound. Had to do two hours guard duty during the night. The carriages have verandahs at their ends where a guard can stand and when the train stopped in the jungle, one could hear the noises of its inhabitants, crickets, lizards, frogs, an echoing cacophony. Fire-flies flew hither and thither.

This is the only track in Malaya and we saw a good part of the country, with countless villages alongside the track. After a time, the scenery becomes monotonous.

The sick quarters are magnificently situated on a white beach...

23rd April 1954
RAF Butterworth
Did my first 'duty orderly' yesterday. There were exercises during the day, and when the siren went, I had to rush into the ambulance and be driven to a point 'in the field' where I stayed armed with first-aid box and stretcher. Airmen, with labels round their necks stating their injuries, were intended to pounce on me and suffer my expert attention, but it suddenly began to pour with rain and everybody retired from the field, sodden.

Last night, I was called out at 3am to help treat a drunken Flight Sergeant with a gash in his head, which he had allegedly sustained from three Malays who attacked him outside the camp. It was thought that, maybe, this was a vision of inebriation...

28th April 1954
RAF Butterworth
...I am digging myself well in here and have completed arrangements for music lessons.

I am taking lessons from a Malayan by the name of Stephen Chin and had my first lesson last Sunday. The Education Officer put him in touch with me. He is a nice, quiet lad and is a teacher and Roman Catholic. He was taught in Liverpool where there is a training college for Malayan students. He has a large studio with many books of good literature and a long-playing gramophone. I heard Brahms Piano Concerto there. In return, he wants me to help him study modern poets and help with English conversation. We started last Sunday with 'Much Ado About Nothing' and I tried to explain some of the archaisms. It will be of great value to me, as my knowledge of literature is rudimentary.

I called on the Headmaster, Mr Wakefield, of the local school in Butterworth, at Stephen's instigation, and will be able to use the school piano in the evenings, so things couldn't be better...

Life is leisurely here; I am on ward duty this week and we have only two patients, so in the intervals I can write letters and songs.

Tried to give an injection in an Indian's arm, but he was so thin and leathery that the needle wouldn't go in. I succeeded eventually.

The MO is a shy, quiet chap who is very conscientious and interested in natural history.

We are situated away from the main camp (thank God) so there is much more freedom here. We can make tea or toast and even indulge in ice-cold lemonade from a fridge whenever we want. We saunter about almost nude. I am getting browner and browner…

24th June 1954
Bidan
The Headmaster tells me that one of the chaps who wrote an article in the Malaya Socialist magazine has been had up for sedition with some others. Mr Wakefield was hoping to get him down to act in one of his productions as he is a good actor. Apparently be had a very stern father. He hates him and this hatred has been transferred to authority – a complex often found among left-wingers.

…This week I am living on an island called Bidan, about half a mile across waiting for 'prangs' of aeroplanes that practise rocket firing on an adjacent island. Usually I wait on a launch near the target, but in the last three days there has been no flying so I have had the days off, enjoying an interesting time on the island. There is a hut with about seven or eight of us and a hamlet with about thirty Indians and a few Chinese who live by fishing. They sing (the Indians) in a monotonous chant as they drag in the net, which contains sting rays, a baby shark, baby octopi and even a globe fish (a picture of which so terrified me when I was a kid).

I saw them beating in the brains of an eight-foot python yesterday which hung from a tree after having eaten some chickens. I ran back for the camera, but was just too late to get an action shot. I've taken one roll and will be sending it to you soon. I visited a cave with bats and felt rather ug-h-rrhy when scores of them flew against my naked torso and brushed me with their furry bums. As we were leaving, the torch happened to illuminate another large python glaring at us from a rocky ledge.

The habitation is over-towered by tall jungle on a hill. Another chap and I attempted to find a path through it to the other side but, after half an hour hacking and sweating, I decided it wasn't my idea of fun (I have never been a boy scout) and we returned.

It is relaxing to roam about almost naked. I am almost burnt sienna colour now, after lying on the deck of a motionless boat.

The camp is run by a Sgt Nobo and is called 'NOBO'S BUTLINS'. A pleasant, elderly chap who slops around in a sarong and, like Gauguin, has gone native. I don't know what he does but he's had a 'bollocking' from the MO who paid him a visit and found the place filthy and the water from the well contaminated. He may have to go.

20th August 1954
Bidan Island
I am on Bidan again for the last time and feel like a roasted pig after a day's sun on the launch to the sound of bombs. One of Butterworth's planes accidentally bombed some of our lads in the jungle, killing three.

The time is towards dusk and I have taken a chair out on the beach (with a stinking cold) to watch the fantastic and lurid sunset that one cannot see in England – burning vermilion, translucent yellow and a creeping oncoming blanket of violet followed by deep night blue. The moon is a ghostly galleon tossed on – all right, skip it. One of those blasted Mambos is now screaming from the billet.

undated
RAF Butterworth
I'm in a very worried state of flux at the moment with my head crammed full of all kinds of things – acting – piano playing – singing – painting – writing – I want to do everything – but as they say 'Jack of all trades…'

I'm working pretty hard in different ways in the evenings.

…Wakefield likes me and we have a lot of discussions; although we are both socialists we often disagree – he doesn't like Picasso or Ibsen. He trembles with hate when he talks about communism, is a great lover of the plays of Bernard Shaw and Shakespeare, is a pessimist about the future of our age and decries films…

2.9.54
RAF Butterworth
Am here today and have just taken orals with two others for S.A.C. exam (senior aircraftsman) and we have passed. However, there is the written to do next Tuesday, which all the others failed last time. I am not that keen to get it, as it occasionally adds extra duties to one's routines when the corporal might be away, but the money would be handy.

[undated, 1954]
RAF Butterworth
…Things 'resting' here at the moment – no plays. Music practice continues steadily – I enjoy it very much – but do you know how far I have to cycle to the piano – there and back? Ten miles! There's enthusiasm for you – in the heat as well. I am going to have a crack at 'The Moonlight Sonata'. I am playing things that become increasingly difficult, and my great trouble is ambidexterity of the fingers.

Stephen, on holiday recently, was arrested as a bandit when walking in the jungle – he said the Home Guard's teeth were chattering and that he (Stephen) thought the guard was a bandit. Some Ghurkas came to S.S.O. a few days ago, shot up a few miles away. Bandits executed an ambush in Penang and killed two police three days ago.

5.11.54
RAF Butterworth
…Latest things on the go are: I am decorating three large rooms in the District Officer's house for the Poppy Day Dance in one week's time – how the hell I'll do it in time I don't know. I am doing a mixture of jungle, underwater scenes, Adam and Eve and Can-Can girls. His wife is very go-ahead and is allowing me to paint on the walls of the house and then they will whitewash it over later if they can't bear to live with it. I start tomorrow with the five-inch brushes and some little girls to help me.

There is also a Poppy Day concert in which I will perform satirical songs at the pianoforte. The rest of the concert will be 'Yeoman of England' and old lady quartets, etc, so it should be like oil and water.

An airman said the other day – 'Oh, John, I enjoyed your song on the radio.'

'That's the first I've heard about it,' I replied.

I don't know whether Rediffusion is trying to do the dirty on me, for they didn't tell me they would be using me. If they don't pay me, I will get the RAF to sue them…

11.11.54
RAF Butterworth
Had dinner with the District Officer and his wife one night and he was telling me of his jungle experiences as he was landed by submarine with the communist guerillas during the war against the Japs. He took the bandit leader to church one Sunday.

21.12.54
RAF Butterworth
…I am afraid I haven't rung up Rediffusion about the fee. Of course there was no contract made. I hate mentioning money matters, but I must tell the old Bastard…

…Mrs Parris, the Warrant Officer's wife, is a character often referred to by others as an 'old cow', as she is fond of scandal. She is a huge woman and will suddenly shout out, 'Hey, Les, stop ballsing about!' or, 'For Christ's sake, sit down on your weary arse!' Being rather domineering, she was booed out of the Families' Club a few weeks ago at a meeting, so I heard. She is very keen on producing variety shows but after performing a strip tease in one show, the CO won't let her do another!

Tonight I am performing at a Naafi Smoking Concert.

Tomorrow evening have been invited to a Sergeant's for drinks.

Tuesday is a private party at Butterworth School, St Mark's.
Am auditioning for 'See How They Run' (camp).
Thursday am going to bed.

25.1.55
RAF Butterworth
How satisfying it is at a quarter past four to devour a quick stodgy tea and go rambling off into the surrounding campus while it is still light. Night falls quickly around seven o'clock and between five and six thirty the sun is hot, but not too hot and it is a pleasant time for a walk to watch the landscape become golden and shadowy as the sun sinks.

A few hundred yards away from SSQ are the wilds. From the gently sloping white, smooth shore, the verge of palm trees and spiky grasses begin which lead to areas of scrub, small allotments and scattered Malay houses. Today I pushed through the scrub and walked on the soft, pastel mauve caked earth of the irrigation ditches; there has been no rain for weeks. Each footfall makes a squelch, betraying the water underneath. Small black crabs dance about even this far inland, mudfish squirm, sometimes lying out of the water – they are like our loach and gudgeon. The countryside teems with hidden life. Constant sharp movements of snakes and lizards skitter through the bushes and grass.

The lizards are like iguanas and are dull orange. I saw a dead one once, about two feet long, which someone caught in the morgue. As one walks, panicking birds rustle out from the bushes, flapping hurriedly away, squawking wildly. The kingfisher is particularly brilliant in its colouring.

Come to a Kampong, and the inhabitants will come out to stare suspiciously, or a worker in a paddy field will give an embarrassed grin. Malay girls hide behind bushes, giggle and run away.

It is a green paradise that one is walking in. The Industrial Revolution has not yet eaten it away.

23.2.55
RAF Butterworth
Had our first corpse the other day. A small shell accidentally went right through an airman's pectoral muscle, and he died on the table as we pumped him with dextrose and blood. So had the job of cleaning him in the morgue...

3.3.55
RAF Butterworth
...Blast Rediffusion! May they go to Hell! No payment or acknowledgement. I am to have a radio series of quarter of an hour programmes on Radio Malaya in April and May, called 'A Young Man's

Fancy' with a couple of songs in each programme. I taped the first one yesterday and received a cheque for 25 dollars, so should get 150 dollars in the end. I shall have to struggle over the piano pieces to get them done in time. Went through my repertoire and am having to cut any sacrilegious or rude words.

4.4.55
RAF Butterworth

We have an epidemic of gastro-enteritis here and the S.Q. is full. I am on duty and am doing more work than usual, looking after eleven patients, and bottling their specimens for examination. So far I haven't caught it.

Two planes crashed and both pilots were killed and once again we had to wash off the fire-extinguisher foam from a charred body resembling a mummy, another with his leg off and a severed foot in a shoe.

25.4.55
Cameron Highlands

Oh for the delights of civilisation (and the mysteries and anguish of love).

I am having a splendid time here – you can't imagine the voluptuous feeling of these last few days of comfort and good company after Her Majesty's Forces.

The Cameron Highlands are ranges of mountains from 4,000-6,000 feet above sea level – heavily covered with trees and for the first time for a year I have been cold and shivered.

'The White House' is on a little hill opposite a golf course and near a hotel – the haunt of colonials needing a rest and a little golf – as I write, these white-panted, pale people below me take putts at little balls and small Indian caddies run to retrieve them.

Here at the house are seventeen people – the Wakefield family – Mr and Mrs Wakefield and their charming daughter and two sons, Chinese girls and boys, Eurasian girls and a few English people…

…the day is spent playing tennis, walking and in the evening, play-reading. The company is charming and we had a little dance last night.

I have met an Eurasian teacher by the name of Alaina de Silva (of English, Portuguese and Chinese origin) – a vivacious girl, and we have gone for long walks talking about art, music and, later last night, after the dance – amour propre. It is the first time that I have kissed lovely lips for over a year.

She left today for her home in Ipoh (100 miles from Butterworth) and so the little romance has ended, except by mail and when we all go to tea at her house on our return journey; she may come to stay at the Wakefield's.

She used to come sketching with me – she studied at the Kirby training college near Liverpool for two years as have most of the people I know.

Now I am a little sad.

Back to the jungle world of death and lunacy – rifle fire rattatats over the hills as our boys have a fight with some newly discovered bandits. Last night I was having a bath when great shells made the house shake and flashes illuminated the night. Round about is a 'black area' and the road up the hills, twisting and turning, used to be famous for ambushes when luckless Europeans were shot.

20.5.55
RAF Butterworth
…I suppose you read of the recent riots in Singapore. Communist infiltration is very powerful there; the young Chinese students almost rule the schools and they and other groups and Unions are ruling by intimidation. A non-communist student was murdered some time ago; the Headmaster of one of the biggest schools in Malaya, in Penang, was murdered two years ago, and, in the recent riots, an attempt to instigate mob-law was attempted even after the newly elected, strongly socialist government had promised to hold an enquiry into the dismissal of workers in the Hock Lee Bus Company. On the riot day, my broadcast had to give way to an emergency speech by the Chief Minister.

undated
RAF Butterworth
…I enclose photos of 'Macbeth' which we are rehearsing, with me in a kind of cowl sitting in front as the porter. Perhaps the best actress was the young girl on the photo marked X who played Banquo's son. She is the daughter of a Chinese prostitute who went mad and the girl is looked after by foster-parents, fisherfolk.

…S.S.Q. work still very quiet with the exception of a potential suicide case whom we guarded for a few hours – an airman who works on a launch, hit another chap and pushed him overboard, tried to ram a junk and then cut his wrist and lay down to die.

I am producing some revue sketches in Penang with another chap and two officers' wives – fast-moving stuff – rather risqué – that will annoy the CO. There is a station Variety Concert soon and the Penang Players are going thru' their birth pangs at the moment trying to launch their first play.

9.7.55
RAF Butterworth
…Next week I've a small part in Penang Players' *Prodigious Snob* by Molière. The Wakefield mob have hired a bungalow on Penang beach where we hope to have a midnight party.

Still struggling with scenery for the Hospital Pageant and have now to do sets for the camp revue.

18.7.55
RAF Butterworth
…Was at the opening of my one-man show in Penang, sponsored by the British Council.

…I mentioned I was 200 dollars up; that is because at a very pleasant preview, in which I was flattered to see perhaps seventy people milling around, I sold six pictures, which adds up to about 200 dollars. Wakefield wanted to buy one but I gave it him in return for his hospitality of the past year. It was 'Moonlit Corridor, Angkor', a photo of which I sent you, among others, in last letter.

Tay Hoi Keat, Arts Association President, bought one, so did an Englishman and another Chinese friend. Mr Mandy of the British Council also purchased one. The whole thing was fun. Afterwards, some of us drove around Penang on the booze.

Oct 1955
…Almost delivered a Malay baby in the ambulance the other night. We rushed to Taiping and the mother had the baby a few minutes after we arrived. Another corpse in; an army national serviceman killed by shrapnel from exploding shell of an artillery section shelling the hills – another chap badly injured with collapsed lung…

…Performed last night at Corporal's dance and the CO has booked me for 'Battle of Britain' dance in the Officers' Mess on the 18th.

26.8.55
RAF Butterworth
Dad, the time has come. You nearly had me home at the end of this week. I was told last night that I was going this afternoon, just a few hours to pack and impossible to say goodbye to any friends, so I complained and managed to wangle a few more days here to give me time for goodbyes, etc. So now am catching train to Singapore on Thursday, September 1st, but don't know when plane will be. You can expect me therefore any time from Thursday 8th September onwards, but will send telegram from England when I know precise date of arrival at the old homestead. Get those b… walls painted and the parsnip wine out. Get the mattress turned and your bowels – er sorry, bowls open.

May hang around Singapore for a few days waiting for the plane. It's like the end of an era.

During my sojourn in Malaya, I went secretly on leave to the temple of Angkor Wat in Cambodia. I love ruins, castles, temples in jungles, et cetera, and after reading Osbert Sitwell's 'Escape with Me' and Norman Lewis's 'A Dragon Apparent', I had to go because I was in the vicinity of the most wonderful ruin in the world.

I enclose some extracts from my diary of the time. (I lost some of it down a storm drain.)

Angkor Wat diary (1954)

The train chugs slowly into Aranya Prathet just after six o'clock and it is growing dark. I stagger away laboriously carting my heavy baggage – a wickerwork case – the handle of which has just snapped. I'm worried about the peg and socket locks that constantly undo, causing a sudden splitting between the lid and the rest of the case that threatens a cataclysm of sweaty vests, books, shirts and this book, which contains my diary, on to the dusty pavement.

The town is ugly and dusty and reminds me of a shanty town. No one speaks English and when I speak and make a gesture of laying my head on my hands in the manner of sleeping, they just smile benignly. Is my mime so bad?

There is nothing approaching a hotel and it is now dark. I am tired, dirty, thirsty and fed up. Oh well, let's try once more – and it works. I am led by a Chinese woman into a shop full of drinking Chinese and follow upstairs through a dilapidated room containing more people having a meal and into an almost completely bare bedroom containing a bed with a dirty sheet and a moth-eaten blanket, a chair and a table upon which stands a big, white jug with a Victorian rose pictured on it. The room leads on to a tiny, rickety balcony that overlooks the main street. I have no alternative but to wash at a filthy basin in the room where the people are eating. The room is oppressively hot whilst I am unpacking and as I begin to sweat profusely I go out to wash. The whole house seems to shake as I tread the boards.

In the middle of my wash, the Chinese woman comes up in a state of anger. I have splashed the water about somewhat liberally and she mutters something to me and mops the floor. Water is dripping on to the café customers below. I feel sorry for causing this poor woman any more trouble, because she looks as if she has suffered hardship; she has an emaciated face with gaunt hollows of the cheek, tired eyes set back in their sockets, and the yellowish parchment colour of skin that comes of years of unbending toil, childbearing and scraping for money.

I escape from the furnace room and go hunting for a café. Who should I see but a boy who I had met on the train. He is able to help me choose and order a tasty meal and I find out the times and procedure for tomorrow before going back to the hovel, which has cooled a little.

Gingerly I lie myself down on the disgusting sheet and soon fall asleep in a pool of perspiration and sense of claustrophobia, my ears assaulted by the intense bustle of Eastern life outside.

The noise is still there when I wake in the morning.

9/11 (collage, 1985, 23 x 34 inches)

Above Señor Cortona Displays an Architectural Caprice
(collage, 1987, 15 x 18 inches)

Right Double Game (3D boxed construction, c1975)

Blue Machine Garden (collage, c1985, 18 x 36 inches)

COLLAGE OF A LIFE XIII

Above Seascape (collage, 1986, 25½ x 33½ inches)

Right Pale Tears
(collage, 1997,
18½ x 22½ inches)

XIV COLLAGE OF A LIFE

Collages from the
'Alice in Wonderland' series, c1980

Above '…*and where have my shoulders got to?*' (13½ x 18 inches)

Above Alice with dentures
(9½ x 13¼ inches)

Below '*Silence every one of you*'
(22 x 18 inches)

Kick Ass (collage, 1991, 8½ x 12 inches)

Eastbourne (oils, 1946)

Lady with Umbrella (oil on hardboard, 1950)

FRIDAY 18TH

The official looks at my passport in the Immigration Office and tells me that I have no re-entry visa into Thailand and that I must go to the Thai Consul in Phnom Penh, the capital of Cambodia, which is over 100 miles beyond Angkor, to obtain one.

'Hell!' I say, and show him my Transit Visa, which the Penang Thai Consul gave me and which he said was sufficient for me to return, through Thailand, on my way back to Malaya.

'No good,' he says.

'What happens if I don't go to Phnom Penh to get one?'

'Well, you can't come back into Thailand.'

'So I stay the rest of my life in Cambodia then?'

'Yes,' the official says, smiling ingratiatingly.

'Hell!'

I drift away, my mind full of black thoughts. This will curtail my stay at Angkor, a stay already limited.

I toss around in my mind various plans and policies as I travel in an old bus to the frontier three miles away. Plans and policies obsess me all day. Shall I come back with the Phnom Penh visa and risk it? The Penang Consul said it was all right. Perhaps the official is mistaken? Perhaps I had better go to Phnom Penh – but Angkor – how many days will I enjoy there? I calculate – two. God! It's a major tragedy. Here am I to see one of the wonders of the world – have come all this way and can see it for only two days Oh, damn it! Let's risk it. But what if they don't let me into Thailand? Then I would be charged by the RAF at Butterworth and might end up in the glasshouse. The RAF don't know I'm here. Does that matter – as we are dealing with a Wonder of the World…?

'No good,' says the official at the border. 'Go to Phnom Penh.'

I stumble off down a dust track to the Cambodian Customs. They tell me my Cambodian Visa is valid for only five days. If I want to extend it, I must go to Phnom Penh.

Blimey! I still stumble on to the railway station of Poipet, cursing.

Today I am making for Battambang for the night. The train, and the country, is full of Cambodian soldiers and a wave of them surges into the compartment searching the passengers' baggage and examining passports.

Through the windows, the country is like a dusty wilderness, flat and deserted, except for occasional kampongs.

A soldier examines a Thai book I am reading on Buddhist sculpture and I exercise a little French.

A cyclocar, the French version of our Malayan trishaw, takes me to the Hotel de la Gare, a slightly more important building than the 'hotel' at Aranya Prathet. This is merely a small house in a row of others, and the sheet is equally filthy and the floor littered with the dog-ends of last night's customers. I attempt to explain that I want a new sheet, but the Chinese woman owner pretends not to understand and brings in the shreds of a towel.

I remember here, especially, the ecstatic throwing off of my sweat-stained garments – the sheer luxury of water from a shower on my body. Kicking the fag ends down the drain in the shower I revelled for several minutes.

I took a stroll looking for a café with French food. The town was ordinary, having something of the French boulevard appearance, with small tree-planted avenues.

I came across a smart hotel that served French meals and ate one at a small table. At the other end of the room sat the United Nations Truce Supervisory Commission, a group of Canadians, Poles and Indians, talking mysteriously.

SATURDAY
Today I was privileged to see one of the wonders of the world; I beheld the mighty mass of Angkor.

Up at 4am I was glad to leave the dingy room of the Hotel de la Gare at Battambang and catch the 5am bus to Siemreap, four kilometres from Angkor.

On arriving at the Grand Hotel and depositing my baggage, I lost no time in jumping into a cyclocar to be pedalled off to the ruins. As I was transported to the temple I had become lost in a reverie – of Henri Mouhot, the French naturalist who discovered the site in 1861.

Slowly, the conveyance wound down the straight road, until, in the distance, I spied the grey walls of the palace. Soon a vast expanse of water came into view, and the cyclocar swung round to follow the banks of the moat, reaching the mustering of soft drinks stalls that clustered at the entrance of the giant causeway leading to the palace.

When I first saw the walls of Angkor peeping from the mass of vegetation, I attempted to imagine the feelings of Henri Mouhot. What a deeply moving experience he must have felt as he suddenly caught sight of grey towers and vast arcades through the thick jungle – the civilisation that a few days earlier he had dismissed in a letter as being an impossibility in such an impenetrable and uninhabited area. What eerie sensations and wonder did he experience as he paced down the long corridors and arcades covered with miles of bas-relief armies surging to war – hundreds of Cambodian dancing girls sculptured at each corner – representations of the life and death, work and play of the ancient Khmer people centuries ago.

As he penetrated deeper and deeper into the grey labyrinth, the sounds of the jungle would have become muffled – the cries of monkeys, the rasp of myriad insects, the growl of some larger animal would have been broken only by the padding footsteps of the explorer and the squeaking of bats. He would have stood amazed, in the silence, regarding the peculiar smile of the Buddha, a smile charged with aloof mystery as the statues meditated on this human being who had broken several centuries of utter solitude.

That was in 1861.

The year is now 1954 and I was drinking a synthetic yellow liquor at a table with an unusually clean cloth – from an unusually clean glass – a little oasis of cleanliness for the tourists.

Having finished my drink I started the long walk along the causeway, past its entrance of broken Nagas, the five-headed snake motifs that constantly rear their heads in the ruins, past the vast pools of still water on either side, where a few small boys dived from the balustrade, past the two Renaissance-like buildings that are believed to have been libraries (the moat only encompasses a certain amount of the causeway), past the square pool covered with waterlilies near the little colony of Buddhist 'bonzes' (priests) that live in neat, wooden huts on stilts and then approached the first flight of steps leading to the main corridor – walls – of the palace.

Through the door one mistily perceives the main bulk of the building with its familiar five towers.

I walked on, climbing higher and higher until I reached the central inner sanctuary, a small chamber containing an image of Buddha and a constantly burning light – the heart of the vast palace. I was alone there.

From here, one may wander at leisure through the endless chambers of this 'Palace of the Orient', admiring the bas-reliefs that fill the walls. These are intricately designed and delicately formalised. The Cambodian dancing girls with their fantastical headgear, elaborate necklaces, bracelets, and skirts, two simple rings round the ankles of their willowy, boneless legs, and protruding rotund breasts, are everywhere. Their faces are the same as the girls I saw today in the town.

Angkor Wat is not really a ruin; it is in a fine state of preservation, and the un-cemented stones are still as solid now as they were when they were built. All the areas of rooms and galleries are small, as they did not use beams and were unable to construct a sizeable roof.

The main inspiration of the Khmer architecture is that of the Hindu in India, but it has an originality of its own surpassing that of India, which is over-decorated and not as refined as Angkor. The figure sculpture too, so blatantly erotic in India, is more chaste and there is no obvious sexuality.

Angkor has many facets reminiscent of other styles. The first impression when one sees the long, symmetrical façade, lakes and moat reminds one of the spaciousness of Versailles. The symmetrical frontage of the palace, with its rising tiers of roofs, square pillars and door are like a place of Renaissance Italy.

The sensation of immovable and enduring greatness that one receives in the presence of certain architecture (Brunelleschi's Church of San Lorenzo in Florence – the cathedral at Seville) is evoked at Angkor.

I would class today's experiences, which have moved me with such peculiar poignancy, with my most memorable moments.

There are sixty square miles of temples! The Bayon, a few kilometres beyond Angkor Wat, is the most strange and original of Angkor's many temples. I do not think it the most beautiful, but it is the most curious.

From some way away it appears as a shapeless mass of facets, and as one nears it, smiling visages are discovered set in the mass of huge, oblong stones that are piled upon each other.

As I wandered among the sixty or more towers, each of which holds four large faces, the sun was sinking and casting sinister shadows on the innumerable facets of the towers, tingeing the grey stone with orange. Silence settled down on the smiling faces that never look at you, but always above you with superiority and supercilious smiles.

Below the towers are corridors and more walls covered in delicately modelled bas-relief, this time devoted, not to the march of armies, but to the domestic life of the Khmers of centuries ago, sculpted with humour and humanism – little incidents such as a person picking the fleas out of a girl's hair – a sight which one sees today, especially in Phnom Penh, where whole families sit on the pavement going through each other's hair… (The rest is lost…)

You will learn that I had visa trouble both getting to Angkor and also returning from it.

Coming back I was arrested at the Cambodian/Thai border for not having the correct documentation yet again. After resting for some hours in the fearsome hot sun, the authorities decided to take me back to Thailand under armed guard, which is a story in itself.

I got back, via the British Consul and the YMCA.

Having crept back into the RAF billet at 4am I snatched a couple of hours sleep. The Sarge hauled me out of bed at 6am when I'd just 'got off'.

He expostulated, 'Come on. Get out of your pit, chuck! You've had bloody three weeks' leave!'

'But Sarge, I haven't had any shut-eye for three days and I feel…'

'You won't sleep for another three days if you don't get up!'

'Bastard!' (I muttered to myself)

He was not a bad old stick, really.

'Owls'

8
Back to school

I had just returned, unannounced, from Malaya and was sitting at our table breathing in the odour of hearth and home. I was eating a boiled egg. My father was slowly milling around adjusting himself to me; I was adjusting myself to him.

A small quantity of smoke issued from an imperfectly laid fire in the grate intermingling with the wafting tang of tipped Senior Service cigarettes.

Circumstances at Number 89 hadn't changed on the incendiary or gastronomic front. The boiled egg was still obviously considered to be my acceptable daily breakfast.

A fit of coughing from both parties now brought us closer together in a more cohesive amalgam.

My father still seemed nimble for his age but thinner. He was still wearing his old trilby and heavily swathed in the traditional muffler worn by him even during the hot flush of summer. For years I had tried to liberate him sartorially but to no avail.

It is touching to remember that he was wearing these very garments when I left for Malaya on that chilly day.

I became more conscious of where I was sitting – I was in the front room again where the Parade passes by – but it looked different. The whole ambience had been jolted.

'What's happened, father?' I asked.

'What's what?' responded my father.

'This room? What's happened?'

'Oh, I've changed it around while you were away. Something to do. New furniture – carpet – rearranged the "Morleys", etc. It looks more lived-in, which in fact it is. The front room is at the back and the back is at the front.'

'Gosh, father.'

'Come and see it. See if you approve.'

We walked off to what we amusingly used to call 'The West Wing'.

I won't commence describing what happened next on this return from

Malaya and its effect on my psyche after the last one and a half years in the tropics...

The front door bell rang...

On the doorstep stood the sprightly, tall presence of Mr Smart, Head Panjandrum of Spencer Secondary Modern School for Boys, which lay opposite the house.

This being September, the term had started, but the school was urgently short of an art teacher with a bit of English and Holy Knowledge on the sidelines.

Though art teachers were never considered of much importance in the educational hierarchy and were regarded as rather comic figures, hopeless at 'discipline', Mr Smart pleaded with me to join the staff there and then.

I would mention here that after one failure, I had gained the Art Teachers' Diploma 'out east' by studying for this certificate of worthiness on Friday afternoons, sometimes taking advantage of the morgue as my study, where it was cooler. I also used it as a studio for art, hoping there would be no sudden arrivals. This was all a bit quick, but I did join the staff that week.

I remember Spencer School being built when I was a boy and the growing of vegetables over the way, which would play their part in 'Digging For Victory'.

I had become a schoolmaster.

I was walking in Dallington Park off the Harlestone Road on the night of November 5th dressed in black drainpipe trousers and red socks, amongst other caprices. I passed a bonfire being built ready for the night. It was swarming with louts from the school. They caught sight of me striding past quicker and quicker and started howling with mirth, me not knowing quite why.

A schoolmaster wearing drainpipes and red socks! A teacher!!! They had all seen the film *The Blackboard Jungle* where Glenn Ford faces a class of East Side kids. The next day I heard a voice in the corridor mutter 'Hi, Teach!', or thought I heard it – not being conducive to one's gravitas. It took some time to settle down after this. I wasn't very good at dealing with it.

In yesteryear, teachers were expected to dress 'straight'. There has been a sea-change in this subject and one can nowadays observe a multitude of styles that eschew 'taste'. Where are the black and chalky gowns of old?

A parent today may well be surprised to meet a young Headmaster with a silver blob fixed to his nostril and a row of bright emerald green spikes made of greased, moulded hair stemming from a bald scalp, or to meet the Deputy Head who has the legend 'SKOOL'S ALL SHIT, MAN' tattooed on his carotid artery.

Forty years ago, on one foolhardy occasion, I acted with the naivety of a young teacher on the assumption that an 'artist' should dress slightly differently and be in touch with the youthful style of the day. I can see now that I had pushed my sense of 'gear' over the edge.

In fact, the school had a reputation for being 'tough' – a bit of a stinker for the young teacher, or for some old ones. The most outlandish noises reverberated from the music teacher's room, where a beat-up old teacher would be wrestling with 4C, a class small in number but enough to drive a teacher to melancholia. (The biggest class sported forty-five souls, if they possessed any souls.) Music was always a risky subject for a vulnerable teacher, laying itself open to aural chaos and dumb insolence ("*e* made that noise, sir'). The emergent singing bore no relation to the western theory of music, as musicians know it, be it tonic solfa or treble clef – more perhaps avant garde. Our Headmaster might be observed hiding in the corridor, peeping into the music room – sometimes entering it and giving the class a hell-fire talking to with a flourish of the cane.

The school suffered a repressive regime. The lid was kept on the boiling kettle too firmly. The cane was always there. The teachers lapsed into cuffing heads and adopted a derisory attitude to the pupils. Was it not our Headmaster who vouchsafed of one 'C' class: 'They're scum.'

I had spent a year at the London Institute of Education where we were fed on a gentle diet of the loveliness of the world and the beauty of 'Child Art' and Marion Richardson. There was little discussion of how to deal with and face the sheer awfulness that pertained in some places. I read the books of A. S. Neil – motivating head of the infamous 'do as you please' experimental school of the thirties and forties, and still with us. 'Neil, Neil, Orange Peel!'

The ethos of Spencer School was certainly abroad. I was gradually sucked into it. I was beginning to absorb the negative elements and, when I look back, am ashamed at my contribution to them.

I visit the immovable nudes

I suffered a further liaison with the New Theatre. In the fifties the Variety Theatre was in its death throes. Northampton's New Theatre had its back against the wall and was driven to presenting shows featuring nudes, who were contracted not to move. The shows had titles like *My Bare Lady*, *Some Like It Nude*, etc, with risqué comic sketches and a blonde, female singer. The police would drop in to check for any movement and then retire to the bar.

I thought I'd visit a show one night as I'd never laid myself open to one and I was firm in the belief that I was out to observe a sociological phenomenon worthy of inclusion in a concentrated study of society's mores.

As I slumped into my seat and settled in the one and sixpennies I heard heavy breathing coming from behind me.

'Hullo, sir,' rasped a voice I knew well.

'You all right, sir?' said another.

'Nice to see you, sir,' and another.

There was a lot of giggling and breaking voices. I wished them all the best and, pretending to be sitting in the wrong seat, looked at my ticket again, rose, and moved to another seat as far away as possible.

The curtain rose and when the nude appeared with tiny bits of the Union Jack adhering to the bottom line, this distracted the boys and, while they were occupied, I thought I'd make a dash for it. But it was too late. There were some more boys sitting on the other side as well who hadn't yet noticed me. I would have to wait for the interval then beat it, which I did, running hell for leather to the nearest beer.

The next day, one of the previous night's boys accosted me in the corridor and said, 'Did you like the theatre, sir?'

'Yes, very educational, Smith,' I muttered, a small group now gathering around me…

There came a rather derisory laugh.

'There's nothing funny about nudity itself, Smithy,' I said. 'Your mothers were nude once and don't you forget it. Now off to the gym and get your clothes off – Mr Edmonds is ill today and I'm taking you for PE. Off!'

An essay in procrastination

If one enters the Spencer School conurbation from the back, which is conveniently placed five minutes walk from my house, one passes the pre-war prefab woodwork hut. Upon turning the far corner one is confronted by a tubular, squat, forbidding erection, constructed from brick and iron reminiscent of one of the chimneys of the five pottery towns, an Ernstian monster or idol, which, if once provoked, might spit into the night hot coals suffusing a reddened sky over St James. My imagination was firing even if the kiln wasn't.

After a firing in this never-never land, I imagined the door would be cranked open revealing cooling ceramic concretions that had started off as once lumpen clay. The boys would be excited by this tactile craft, especially if their pots remained still in one piece! A lot of broken hearts here.

This kiln was the brainchild of Mr Smart, conceived by him and constructed with help from the boys. Erstwhile educationalists, art teachers and pedagogues from Northampton and its shires made pilgrimages to this admirable pillar of educational enterprise and the kiln was duly shown off to their wonderment.

As the new art master, the Head took me round the school, completing our tour opposite the kiln. Mr Smart stood there and beamed. It was already some years old. I remarked that the construction appeared to have a surprisingly new patina.

'Ah,' said Mr Smart. 'We're now preparing for "The Big Day",' and, eyeing me benignly, said, 'This is where you come in. We're on our way! Perhaps we could synchronise it with Open Day – if we have one.'

Then reality hit me and I thought, 'Oh, blimey! I'll have to hone up on my ceramic techniques as I've got a little rusty, so to speak.' I had dabbled in pottery on the teachers' course at London University but didn't enjoy it.

Months passed as I settled in until the day when I began to think that perhaps it really was time to have a go at trying out the kiln.

From time to time art teachers and educationalists from the county and town evinced interest in the project and asked if there were any developments.

Slightly embarrassed, I'd tell them, 'We're on our way! We're now preparing for the Big Day! Have a drink, if you're free.'

Boys would enquire what was happening. Every few months I would approach Mr Smart's office with a suggestion that we could give the kiln a whirl. In negative response he would explain the various unfortunate financial and mechanical problems inhibiting the launching of this elemental force.

I taught for four years. Many years later I was passing by the Spencer Academy for young gentlemen, as we sometimes called it in merry mood, and saw an open door. I knew then where I had to go. Impelled by nostalgia, I found myself padding down the corridors, observed by suspicious teachers, towards the woodwork hut. I turned the corner, somehow knowing what I was going to see. There rotted the unused kiln, now weather-worn with crumbling brickwork and textured
with obscene graffiti.

Mr Smart had died long ago I heard…

I would suggest that this kiln should be nominated as a monument to the above late Headmaster.

It became known as Smart's Folly.

Stand up Conroy Maddox

One day I said to my wife-to-be Julia, a voluptuous art teacher whom I had met whilst supply teaching in a Catholic Secondary Modern School in Walthamstow, 'Let's go hunting sonofabitch surrealists along the south coast of Great Britain. There are a few holed up here and there, I hear.'

Already we knew Conroy Maddox from the sixties, a collagist and last of the old school, who had met the original surrealists in Paris and who had spent the war in Birmingham as a commercial artist. He now lives in Hampstead, collaging in the photo-montage style. He had kindly given us a Christmas present in the shape of a collage featuring a nude nun. He was haunted by the concept of the seduction of nuns, and the local convents had to be notified when he was in the area.

Stand up John Banting

After a certain amount of preparation for this bivouac, we travelled down in Julia's red Morris Post Office van to a safe house (public) in Hastings and were told that if we played it cool we would definitely bump into Banting, a paid-up surrealist old-timer and acerbic communist (CPGB), who was likely to be found under the influence of Opening Time.

Sure enough, we caught him cutting a vitriolic dash as a barrack room lawyer in a very smoky, crowded bar near the esplanade on this hot Saturday afternoon.

We introduced ourselves and Banting, breaking off his cut-and-thrust with the bar room bar flies, listened to our explanation that I was none other than the son of the Compte de Lautreamont in person and that the lady by my side was the sister of Lop Lop Superior of the Birds. (Ref: Lop Lop was the alter ego of Max Ernst.)

'Don't try and be funny with me,' riposted Banting, thrusting a forefinger at me upon which he sported a spiky ring that nearly lacerated my cheek.

'Do you know what this is for? It's to beat *squares*, but anyway, have one on me,' and he bought us half a pint each.

I think he was flattered that he, a forgotten artist, had been tracked down by surreal aficionados on a pilgrimage.

Through the alcoholic haze and the shrieking of seagulls he spoke of his life history – starting as a bank clerk – studying Art in Paris, where he met the French Surrealists, who else? Joining the English group later and taking part in the big International Exhibition in 1936 in London at the Burlington Galleries – designing decor for ballets, murals and book jackets – during the war working as Art Director on documentaries and official films…

Then it was 'Time, gentlemen, please,' and as we said our goodbyes he said with a snarl, 'My life history is best forgotten. Have another one on me…'

Within a few months he had died.

Sit down Ithell Colquhoun

We thought we'd better push on to the next surrealist who laboured under the name of Ithell Colquhoun and lived in Cornwall.

After some correspondence we tracked down Ithell Colquhoun in her quaint cottage in Penzance, a friendly person who chuckled and laughed whilst offering Typhoo tea and cupcakes served on a silver tray in the manner of a Miss Marple.

She was pleased to meet us and tell about the ramifications of English Surrealism at the time of the war. (In her exhibition in Cork Street she exhibited a live tramp sitting in the window – not pickled in formaldehyde, as is the present fashion, but au naturelle.)

When I mentioned the name of the Big Chief Tonio del Renzio – wasn't he a bit of an objectionable cad? – she burst out with a cackle, 'That was my husband!'

A division had occurred in the ranks of the English group. E.L.T. Mesens, the other boss (whom you may remember from earlier on in these pages), set out some demands that the party line should follow in the imperious manner of André Breton. Ithell Colquhoun refused to subscribe to it and left the group. Tonio del Renzio was very committed to Surrealism but his association with her damned him in the eyes of E.L.T. and a typical feud ensued in the traditional surrealist manner.

> 'In the late 1930s, when Surrealism had arrived in England, Ithell Colquhoun was one of the young artists whose works were being exhibited in the progressive galleries of London, and her reputation as a serious artist and explorer of the real and unreal has remained throughout her artistic and literary development.' (Catalogue quote)

But the break with the party pushed her more and more to the realm of the occult and alchemy and she became a member of a mystic group of artists from Belgium called Fantasmagie.

A writer and poet, Ithell Colquhoun wrote a dreamlike picaresque novel called *Goose of Hermogenes*, which contains the archetypal Gothic images – the Grail – a castle – a strange silent factotum – sex ghosts – a sinister Uncle – and while we talked of birth and death the subject of fertility came up. Later, when Julia and I had been married for some time, we tried to procreate, but to no avail, resulting in Julia's growing sadness.

The possibility of my own infertility had been investigated by an elderly consultant, an authority on the subject, who told me that, as far as he was concerned, he was the Pope. The treatment was to splash the goolies with ice-cold water twice a day and wear pants that were floppy and not too tight in the nether regions – what we call jockey shorts and are fashionable now. Some actresses inadvertently once saw me dressing backstage in Kidderminster and from then on I became known as 'Droopy Drawers'.

The theory is that heat causes infertility and one must keep it away from the seminal area. I have only two million sperms with a short sell-by date, but one needs a sharp eighty million to do the job properly and apparently mine have weak heads and can't even move it on the super-seminal highway. A little op didn't help.

Ithell, after hearing our story, suggested we visit a source of psychic energy some way away. Putting on her boots and steadying herself with an umbrella, she took us on a long journey to the bare moors and rocks, miles from her cottage, to a remote area on which stood a dolmen with a hole in it, formed rather in the manner of the late Henry Moore, and wide enough for a human body to crawl through. By now we were exhausted. Ithell informed us that this was a spiritual place emanating a force of sheer fertility and, in an increasingly imperious manner, she commanded Julia to take off her clothes and crawl naked through the aperture. Julia, who never suffered from false modesty, did as she was bid and wriggled through it as lissom as a snake-hipped Cleopatra. I don't exaggerate (and would never like to be accused of this vice), but at that moment a low, yellow fog was slithering slowly towards us from the distant sea. Ithell, her face paling in anticipation of there being some danger in finding our way back, counselled Julia to dress quickly and we fled from this mystic haunt.

It was soon after this brush with the pagan world that I was pronounced highly infertile by the ancient oracle in the North London hospital. But should one put one's faith in a consultant who labours under the delusion that he is the Pope?

Some time later I played the Reverend Quiverful in David Giles's BBC production of *The Barchester Chronicles* by Trollope. The Reverend gentleman was indeed a gentle man, ever meek and ever mild; ironically for me, this benign character is blessed with fourteen children. I meditated on the irony that had granted my fictional character the fatherhood of all these proliferating children yet my real self remained bereft of offspring.

When I first met Julia whilst teaching in Walthamstow I was also acting in the evenings in a West End show – juggling two balls at a time, so to speak. She had been recommended by my RAF friend, Kirby Green, as a teacher.

Having the wild looks of a Calabrian Madonna, Julia could be good fun and saucy with it; at other times I called her 'La Tempesta', but, excuse her, please – she came from a highly disturbed background. The root of it?

Vegetarianism – her saintly parents were dyed-in-the-wool vegetarians, almost vegan in their fundamentalism, and were obsessed with serving their famed 'Soya bean stew' à la 'Sandy Point', which they served nightly to their ravenous guests. They managed a mock-Tudor vegetarian guest house in Frinton-on-Sea, which was known as 'Sandy Point'.

Their advertising logo was 'It's lentil lickin' good!' (am I jumping somewhat?), but, nevertheless, to be on the safe side, I would take my own tuck box when I went down for weekend short stays. On such occasions, when suffering from insomnia, I would roam the corridors and notice a guest rifling the refrigerator for some items to make up a 'Midnight Feast' – sausages and meat balls belonging to a non-vegetarian spouse.

During an argument, rather than licking me, Julia once bit me on the hand outside a police station whilst in charge of agricultural machinery and an opened bottle of 'La Dolce Vita'.

Our friend, Kirby Green, helped me to hide her from several constables who burst out of the station, hearing an altercation.

I still have that scar.

Brutal!

When people enquire how I hurt myself, I pretend the wound was sustained during one of my sorties in the Malayan jungle; obtained in action, you know!

Frinton is no Clacton. Nor Jaywick Sands. But this town holds a rudimentary theatre that was once a Boy Scouts' hut.

I had previously enquired of the theatre management whether it would undertake to put on my vegetarian version of *Macbeth* with a publicity campaign based at 'Sandy Point', but, owing to procrastination, I was merely asked to give vocal body to a sing-song 'Down Memory Lane' at the local nursing home.

We had tried to get married in Turkey.

After a three-day journey across Europe (most of that time being taken up by the slow locomotion of Bulgarian Railways – beards off, by the way), burdened with baggage and easels and having been gently stoned by urchins, which seemed to be a common practice there towards tourists, we reached the flat overlooking the Bosphorus owned by an English lady spy (with a friend of a friend in MI5), whose address had been given to us.

This lady, who spoke Turkish, took us down the next day to get information from the appropriate dingy office, which would clarify this matter of a Turkish marriage.

Our spy explained the situation and the surly official welcomed us.

'Passport!' he snarled.

Our spy friend asked for more information, please, before releasing the valued document. We were grudgingly informed that we would have to stay in the country for six weeks to establish residence. I began to feel like the sick man of Europe.

So that was it (in Turkey), as Julia had to be back at work before then.

At this time I was fascinated with filming Standard 8mm 'home movies', of something a little more advanced than pictures of babies on the lawn, a pleasure we lacked.

But here, in the centre of Anatolia, Turkey boasted a remarkably photogenic landscape, which we had planned to visit.

In Goreme, the valley is one of the most extraordinary in the world – modelled by Nature in dazzling, powdered white soft tuff that has been twisted into towers, caves and a thousand dovecotes – eaten away by the centuries, reminiscent of the architecture of Gaudi.

I was using this weird, fairy-tale landscape as a setting for an experimental home movie about St Jerome. The landscape is hollowed with the troglodyte cells of anchorites and mystics and intimate shrines cut from the soft rock with frescos of the Christian imagery still existing. St Jerome was one of the hermits who lived there.

In one epistle he reflects, 'In the remotest part of the wild and stony desert burnt up with the heat of the scorching sun so that it frightens even the monks that inhabit it, I seemed to be in the midst of the delights of the Roman maidens – my will felt the assaults of desire.'

It was here, in this haunted setting, with the ghosts of holy hermits, that I wanted to take a few shots of Julia, nude, emerging from a cavern, surrounded by sunflowers, representing 'The Phantom of Desire'.

Initially, she was rather 'cheesed' at the concept and began feeling tired.

'Oh, not again!' she whimpered. But eventually she cooperated, negotiating the rocks most daintily, heightened in my lens by a few colour filters. Unfortunately she jumped occasionally, having made painful contact with a thorn.

She would certainly have appeared enticing to any anchorite, swinging his rosary, who might have stumbled in her path.

And that day I forgot her birthday – uh-uh!!! All day she was waiting for the traditional greeting – it never came.

When we got the home movie back to England and developed it, Julia appeared invisible. The filters had wiped off her image: Zap! Zap! The scenes had become a psychedelic vision, which, I suppose, was appropriately mystic.

After further exploration of this Ottoman land, upon finding ourselves short of money, we fled from the countryside to the railway station.

Julia had had enough! Six weeks in the cheapest of 'hotels' because of lack of money, we were also due back for teaching commitments. Those were the days of Harold Wilson and one could only take abroad £60 per person maximum (according to exchange/control regulations).

We had painted quite a few works – Julia's were no oil-painting, but then she was using gouache. I chose oils; using this medium in a desert resulted in their surfaces being encrusted with white tuff, pleasantly textured.

We had beaten off a few more stonings by delinquent urchins but one gentleman offered to kill me when we refused to attend a rather sinister-sounding party. I must say that Johnny Turk is extremely friendly, but it's best not to cross his path.

Was there something about me?
Was there something about Julia?
Now it can be told.

'Tomb View'

We married, soon after this, in Hampstead Registry Office and stayed in Parliament Hill, at the house of two of the Barrow Poets, whilst we looked for a house to buy. We found our dinky Wendy House in East Finchley, which we christened 'Tomb View' – our grounds abutted a graveyard, the St

Pancras and Islington Cemetery. This little suburb of East Finchley, this demi-Paradise, this…?, was frequently featured on radio in *The Goon Show* and used as a metaphor for mirth.

EFNA

Fairly soon after having staked out our territory to the tune of £3,200, a furore arose in the vicinity, stimulated by the East Finchley Labour Party, over a threat to widen the East Finchley High Road. This perceived future leviathan gave birth, in its turn, to a Neighbourhood Association – all the fashion at that time in the seventies.

We attended an inaugural meeting in the library and joined in the mood. From then on we met and made friends by the score with all types of homo sapiens: Conservatives, Labourites, Liberals, revolutionaries, followers of Findhorn, mad doctors, Jehovah's Witnesses, Trotskies, ne'er-do-wells – possibly one hundred people became members.

After an EFNA meeting we might repair to the nearest pub, a very small relic of the 1940s run by a surly landlord and gentle wife.

Too many of us would swamp the elderly indigenous denizens of the pub. When advised that an East Finchley Neighbourhood Association group was on its way, His Grumpiness would seize up and mutter 'EFNA?! You mean *EFF OFF* DONCHA?' which some did. However, some hardened sociologists didn't.

We found ourselves helping old ladies across the road – giving them advice on how to get back again – clearing ponds of supermarket trolleys – attending concerts, belly dancers, poetry recitals (in pubs), ladies' football matches and organising events for OAPs (which inevitably I have now joined, disillusioned as I became with the Boys' Brigade!).

Now, all has vanished – those joyful times, those dear people.

I walk up the East Finchley High Road alone now, rarely meeting any of those gentle people who were there. Many have moved. Many have died. The treasurer was murdered outside East Finchley station. The flyover (which we delayed for fifteen years at public enquiries) now roars away 'up and running'… Even Julia has vanished.

      Fumms bo wo taa zaa Uu
          pogiff
                    kwii Ee

    dii rrrrrrr beeeeeee   bo fununs bo wo taa
                                bo fumms bo wo taa zua
                                bo fumms bo wo taa zua Uu

The 'Ur Sonata' by Kurt Schwitters – artist, collagist, typographer, concrete poet, sculptor, comedian, Dadaist. His characteristic works are the many tiny pictures built up with detritus scavenged from the world's epidermis – bus tickets, stamps, hair, string and newsprint – which all take on a jewel-like quality, and sometimes a severe elegance.

He was an artist who influenced me throughout the years. He began life as an expressionist in the spirit of sturm und drang, but became caught up in the Dada movement in Berlin with its disgust for the horror and tragedy of the First World War.

The Berlin Dadaists attacked him for being too 'bourgeois' and not politically correct, so he returned to his home in Hanover in the twenties where he conducted his own form of Dada, which he called 'MERZ' – a chopped up nonsense word cut arbitrarily from a newspaper.

In Hanover he built his first Merzbau, a giant inhabitable collage that he expanded until it filled the room and grew through the ceiling, to his good lady wife's chagrin. It was bombed to bits in the war.

He fled to Norway from the Nazis and built a Merzbau there. Children burned it down whilst 'playing with matches'.

He finally escaped to Britain. He was interned for a year in a camp at Douglas, Isle of Man, where he found himself amongst the incarcerated intelligencia and never stopped collaging. He was released. E. L. T. Mesens gave him a show and he started working on his third Merzbau in Ambleside, which was transferred, when he died in 1941, to Newcastle Art Gallery, where it remains.

Out of respect for my glue-bound mentor I have made two pilgrimages to Schwitters sites – first to Douglas, Isle of Man, to see the camp site on which he was interned. His quarters were in Hutchinson Square, now once again restored as a seaside boarding house plying its polite trade opposite a neat, formal park, which once heard the sound of boots and the clash of eating irons and foreign languages. The day we visited was damp and dull. No one in sight. I stood, saluting and letting loose an introductory howl, then proceeded to give forth a rendition of another poem in Kurt's Concrete Golden Treasury:

> lanke tr q'
> pe pe pe pe pe
> ooka ooka ooka ooka
> tanke tr ql
> pll pll pll pll pll
> zuuka zuuka zuuka (Did Caxton come to this?)

As the notes stopped, my ears became very alert. Not a sound was heard. Not a foonerial note. No curtains were disturbed by a peeping observer. The guests were fast asleep. Was I wasting my time? My companions, Joan and her cousin Elaine, had moved on.

My other pilgrimage was no trouble. The site is a ten-minute walk away from Joan's flat in Barnes, where, halfway down Chesterfield Road, is a blue plaque with the legend 'KURT SCHWITTERS LIVED HERE'.

This time it was a sunlit Sunday morning. Again the street was empty. I stood near the front gate of the home where he and his muse and friend 'Wante' ('Want tea?' Get it?) had lived briefly and delivered a recitation of a fragment of the 'Ur Sonata'.

This time there were slight disturbances at several windows. I stopped. Still the road remained empty, front doors shut. There must have been nervous discussions among those who had risen to watch as to the best way of approaching this phenomenon. The police or hospitalisation? I walked away.

I can only surmise that the British public is not yet ready for my street performances of Schwitters in Barnes and the Isle of Man.

My third pilgrimage, and I suppose my last, will be to the tomb in Ambleside where Schwitters is buried.

Besides his sounds, I have lived half a century in the Wonderful World of Collage here and there, up and down, man and boy, and this is the artistic style that suits me best.

Many people ask me, 'Mr Adams, sir, what is collage?'

I tell them in the simplest manner I can muster: 'My friend, when two bits of paper are stuck together in his name (Schwitters) then I say unto them, this, thus, is collage.'

Kurt said, just before he died, 'fumms bowo taa zua.' I wouldn't demur from this statement.

I was in the Tower Records shop recently when Joan said excitedly, 'Jonathan, come over here!'

I went over and saw a compact disc recording the whole of the 'Ur Sonata' performed by Schwitters himself in 1946.

The number was WER 6403-2.

'Owls'

9
Acting

'Let's get this show on the road'

At the age of twenty-eight I decided to become an actor.
I told my father.
'You bloody fool!' he said.

I'm sure he was secretly pleased – my father could be very 'theatrical' at times, even embarrassingly so, when he was happy, and I have perhaps three hundred original postcards of his creative life in the prison camp in Munster where he lingered throughout the Great War. I have copies of the camp newspaper he edited and contributed to; he was an excellent cartoonist; arts and crafts exhibitions were staged, and concerts.

He performed music-hall songs and sketches in the surprisingly sophisticated theatre the prisoners had constructed behind the wires, so they now queued for entertainment besides the necessity of queuing up for watery soup and mouldy bread, and they had the additional task of delousing the hand-sewn costumes before their return to wardrobe.

In fact, he and his fellow performers gave quite literally lousy performances. It was possibly my father's most creative period in this prison camp.

It was time to prepare and prove myself, me, an untrained country boy, for my date with Showbizniz. The inspirational moment could strike at any time and one had to be steady and ready, bright-eyed, tail as bushy as a whippet's on a hot tin roof, or they just wouldn't look at you. I was working on stage technique and studying to become a master of the double-take. My neck snapped but righted itself. I had already given Carol Levis his chance.

I prepared myself with two audition pieces as is the wont, one by Shakespeare – Puck in *A Midsummer Night's Dream* (no typecasting there, aha!), and the other Long John Silver in *Treasure Island*.

I chose the latter because a West End company used to invite auditions for it annually at Christmas time and I could kill two birds with one stone. *Peter*

Pan at the Scala was *out* as far as I was concerned. Whimsy. Failing that, a producer might see me as a basic pirate – quite a few were needed then.

Don't cry, 'Cliché! A palpable cliché!' when I say that Silver is a monumental role. I've always felt that I could bring something more to the part than did the late Sir Bernard Miles. His handling of the declining parrot was woeful and his cry, 'Aa ha aah arrrr – Jim Lad!' was vulgar in the extreme.

The essential item in one's theatrical armoury is, of course, plenty of carefully posed photographs to send to the agents – a fearful lot, apparently – whose names and addresses are contained in a book entitled *Contacts*.

The photographs are featured in a biblical-sized volume called *Spotlight* where hundreds of actors reproduce their faces in an ill-assorted line-up – prisoners of their aspirations. This was costly, so I thought I'd approach one of my Northampton Players' chums to do some for me on the cheap.

After a few days I was asked to collect them from his small studio. I could just make out that the dark room was festooned with innumerable identical photographs of myself looking broody – in fact, there were, literally, a thousand prints of my visage suspended from the ceiling and, well, everywhere. Unintentionally it appeared that I had grossly over-ordered, a combination of his deafness and my deafness had resulted in a thousand rather than a hundred prints being produced.

As I limped out, shuddering and light of pocket, one of the technicians muttered after me, 'He thinks a lot of hi'self don' he?'

I still have a few hundred of these now rather valuable and historical pieces of nostalgia in my keep. I store them in a needlework basket. Those that were loosed upon the theatrical world proved sterile. It took me some time to pay my debts. Though I have tried to interest fish restaurants in the West End, they say that their walls are full.

If any reader feels emboldened to request a free print for his/her collection, I will be pleased (on receipt of a SAE) to forward one, asap (DV).

I had handed in my pedagogic notice to Spencer Secondary Modern School for Boys and set out on my journey to The Wicked City carrying my copy of *An Actor Prepares* and sticks of Leichner Numbers 5 and 9 on the long haul to fame. This took me a year, getting nowhere.

I continued to earn my keep by embarking on part-time or supply teaching for two days a week, staying with friends. Many assorted posts I was to fill. I quivered on the edge of stardom. 'SCHOOLMASTER ON SUPPLY IS AN OVERNIGHT SENSATION!' I would dream… 'Macbeth on Supply'… My first peripatetic teaching engagement was in a very small private academy in suburban Pinner, being paid at a reduced rate.

The Headmaster of this set-up was a corpulent, quiet, elderly buffer who kept himself to himself and who had pared down the expenses of the school to a minimum with a view to dissolution.

The Science Block comprised several test-tubes, a bunsen burner, a quantity of cobalt sulphate, and iron filings, which would be returned to a cupboard after the experiment had been performed.

The books were dog-eared to say the least. *Pilgrim's Progress* reared its head once more. The Bibles and hymn-books were stacked in teetering piles like the stones of Gormenghast in the hall corner, which had come to be known as 'The Librarium'.

The available art materials consisted of A4 white cartridge paper and a limited selection of HB pencils, greasy crayons, shiny-skinned india rubbers and warping rulers. The backs of the used drawing sheets were to be used again.

If the Headmaster applied a cane to a boy he gave him a hug afterwards in commiseration, so it was said.

The three Gormenghastian teachers engaged by this academy, besides myself, were first a sun-kissed, boyish physical jerker from Australia, very popular as most PE teachers are, second, one whose mind wandered the periphery of the occult and had a strange son who was apparently blessed with the Third Eye, the father often telling us in the Common Room or at lunch break that the boy was the repository of an arcane knowledge. This teacher was at loggerheads with the third teacher, a vegan fundamentalist with a refined glossy cranial bone structure and flowing silver locks, like a suburban Krishnamurti who kept himself up an ivory tower

I once offered him a sausage roll and he snapped back, 'Aye don't eat *corpse*, thenkyou,' and returned to reading *The Vegan Book of Jokes*. He brought in his own Spartan veggie-fare, which was probably the sensible thing to do in the gastronomical circumstances. Our school dinners normally consisted of two small taut-skinned sausages, an accretion of 'Wonder' mashed potato, sad, striated vegetables, followed by spotted dick and a glass of thinned orange juice. It has even been known for the Headmaster to do the cooking when the usual source of culinary activities was indisposed.

After my spending one term there, a new Headmaster took over. He was a brusque ex-Army officer, out and about, ubiquitous: 'I'm on the war path, lad. Stand up straight, boy!' Thus would he lard the atmosphere with commands and strictures useful for a possible invasion or for the future battle of life: 'Manners Maketh Morals'.

More progressive than his predecessor, he let me pin up reproductions of works of this 'Modern Art' in the corridors: Van Gogh's 'Sunflowers' ('A bit *loud*, Mr Adams, eh?'). He 'shook up' the academy somewhat. His wife cooked the school dinners. Better! The Brussels sprouts were better. Better batter, baking-wise.

In the Common Room he once, rather apologetically, mentioned that a Hitler rally he had accidentally attended before the war was undoubtedly 'rather stirring', before we knew about 'these things that happened'.

He supported me in the playing, at assembly, of records of suitable 'cultural music' with a brief spoken introduction to the pieces. The Headmaster wanted to play a snatch from Wagner but I commenced by letting loose with Saint-Saens's 'Danse Macabre', which went down well – the original inspiration of my little number 'Stompin' at the Graveyard Ball'. The Headmaster was worried when I asked if I could give an after-hours lecture on jazz.

'Be careful to keep it decent, Adams, and not too silly,' he advised.

The Headmaster's support waned when I got the boys to cover the playground with paint. They had seen on television 'A mad artist, sir. A nutter, sir,' whose metier was creating abstract form by wheeling a bicycle with paint-covered wheels over a surface. I brought in several tins of powder paint and explained that art is not just mindlessly copying flowers with a brush. As colourful arabesques began to take shape on the tarmac, the bicycles were doing their aesthetic work when the Headmaster emerged somewhat perturbed. I had to explain 'What for jolly heaven's sake was going on!' I tried to.

It was not only the teachers that were unique when I was 'on supply', but the bricks and mortar of my next post, an independent school.

My second educational position was housed in an eccentric building in Wandsworth that appeared to overhang a railway cutting and I taught in this vast, Town Hall-like mansion, an early Gothic 'open plan', with myriad locked rooms and halls, cupboards and corridors, disappearing into a gloomy nether world that had once been used as a hospital for survivors of the Crimean War. Once I thought I heard the faint howling of wounded ghosts – but – I slapped my wrist. How silly. Its dark and ghoulish grey towers and echoing vaults were infested with flapping bats in the rafters, which would swoop down in the middle of a biology lesson, and scuttling rats in the cellars. The school's working area seemed to fill only one small part of this vast edifice and was, as it were, an enclave that still functioned as a school.

After a lesson had commenced, because of odd architectural angles, it was easy for a boy to disappear into the shadows unnoticed, read a book, or escape into the light.

From a school that had been deemed 'Crimean Independent', the authorities were trying to bring it forth into the late nineteenth century. Thus 'Gothic Comprehensive' was one of the educational experiments that were taking place about this time.

I believe that now the building is used by 'Super Burger Boy'. Scrumptious!

This is Showbizniz

'uM ah!' said Brian Way, children's theatre producer and progressive educationalist in his incredibly low-slung voice. 'Thank you, Jonathan, very nice, uM. I like what you did. We would like you to join the company for uM one school term next month, umM. We would like to give you a salary of uM seven uM pounds uM a week.'

Suddenly I was pitched into Showbizniz – Showbizniz??? Was this Showbizniz? Acting, nay, cavorting, to lots of kids all over the country by van? I soon got to know that one could learn a lot about acting during such school performances – how to animate forty-five rough toughs, who had previously been farting – or worse – and melt their hearts. We performed a play about Elizabeth Fry, the heroic woman who brought succour to the prisoners of Newgate and tried to reform the penal system. During the performance the audience would find themselves being drawn into the drama, forgetting their previous resistance. Scenes were built into the script where the pupils could join in the action (prisoners in Newgate, soldiers, officials, etc), which they did with great sincerity. Brian Way would visit us to see that all was not chaos. 'UmmM…'

Showbiz – there I was! I completed a term with Brian and hoped to read an advert in *The Stage* offering a role for a 'fledged actor' who didn't have to sweep the floor, stay up all night to help paint the scenery, prompt, get the coffee, get the tea. I did not know that straight actors never got a job through writing to *The Stage*, but only tall, lovely showgirls graced with exceptionally long legs.

I took a post at Preston with The Century Theatre, assuming the job was for your proper actor, but, when reading the programme, found that I was still listed as an ASM (Assistant Stage Manager – in years gone by, most actors had to start their career in this humble position). The manager, John Ridley, was an enterprising, humane individual. He offered me an extra £1 a week if I'd stay on, to which I agreed. I asked the manager if he would employ my girlfriend, Vilma, an actress, very beautiful and oversensitive, whom I met with Brian Way as an ASM. Again the manager agreed. However, one of the directors couldn't get on with her and she was sacked. I repeated, therefore, that I too would leave. However, the troubles were resolved and life continued. All this argument took place under canvas. Why? The theatre was situated in a tent.

I shared one room in digs with another actor. One night this gentleman did not return. When I awoke I noted that his bed was empty. I realised, instinctively, with whom he had spent the night. This time I did leave. It was the first time I was really hurt and jealous.

The last time I was an ASM was with David Scace in the Library Theatre, Manchester. The ASMs there usually played good parts. David Scace was an imaginative, if rather frightening director who called you 'darling' even though he was a red-blooded male. I seemed to be underground all the time in 'The Stacks', working like a Nibelungendwarf but one less vertically challenged. I was so tired that, after bringing down the final curtain one night, I took it up again. The actors were transfixed, caught in mid-action, and froze, smiling slightly. Then I brought it down again. Then up. Then down. I was fast losing my grip.

The Stage Manager, John Franklyn Robbins, shouted, 'Bring whoever is responsible to me *now*!!'

My fellow ASM was a certain Anthony Hopkins. Tony didn't hit it off with the powers that be and eventually left in Welsh dudgeon after decapitating several score of light bulbs in the dressing rooms.

After six months at Manchester in the winter, it was some relief to go 'down south' and dabble in the summer season at Ilfracombe, where we executed three plays in the evenings and swam in the afternoons. I also drew in the daytime – recalling memories of Bexhill, it's Variety Theatre, brass band, harbour and rude postcards.

My perpetually dank and moist bedroom was separated, by a cracked window only, from a sheep dip, which I appropriated as a studio, all at a very reasonable price. A fellow actor bedded next to the dip and proceeded to snore every morning away, which led me to the application of cotton wool as a silencing agent.

It was a sepulchral summer. Weather so-so. I wish you had been there. To be young was so very heavy…

We mounted, for a further four days, a production, of Harold Pinter's *The Caretaker*. It was not entirely to the liking of the now dwindling holidaymakers. We only just learned the words in time.

The Lionel Hamilton Experience

It was soon after I had packed up my sheep-dipped art impedimenta and made my way back to Northampton that I received a call from Lionel Hamilton, the director of the Northampton Theatre Royal (a charming Victorian building), usually referred to as 'The Rep'.

Lionel asked me if I would join the company and play in *Salad Days*. 'Look at me: I'm dancing! Ooo Ooo!' I was thrillllled and said, 'Yep, please.'

I was to remain with the company for three years 'doing fortnightly' under Lionel's baton.

In passing, I noted that Errol Flynn, a one-time company member, had left long before me and had become known for his hell-raising proclivities in our sleepy town. He went on to Hollywood where he specialised in swashbuckling roles and a life of hideous debauchery, or so I hear.

Now retired, Lionel had been at the theatre since 1947, first as an actor then director. I knew him socially from earlier Northampton days when I was a student in the local arty world there.

Those three years of enjoyable 'fortnightly' now leave me with many nostalgic memories – performances of varying quality – some that still make me blush.

Saturday night's second house could be nightmarish, especially if an Agatha Christie thriller had to be got through twice before 10.45pm with the senior character lady essaying (as they say) Miss Marple. The ASM on the book had to be especially alert, as indeed did the surrounding actors, after she had 'been out between shows'. The denouement, when the inspector (sometimes me) had to interrogate the lady at length, sometimes found her wanting in clarity and logic and, whilst fiddling with her trug, she had to be guided gently to various marked points on the stage, which were bright yellow so she could see them. This would be accompanied by a lowering of the emotional temperature in the audience.

One fine evening at the Rep, I had completed my characterisation of the Squire in Emlyn Williams's *The Corn is Green* and, having time to spare before the final curtain, I thought I'd climb up into the flies and watch this educative Welsh drama from above.

Clambering discreetly up the steel, rattling ladder, I reached the top and, looking for a vantage point from which to watch, it seemed strangely quiet on the stage below. I looked down and, besides noting an ill-fitting wig-join on the top of the head, observed that the two characters were transfixed, as if frozen, uttering a halting stilted dialogue that I failed to recognise. Was it Welsh? The performance of Miss Moffatt, the teacher, and her 'Emlyn Williams' look-alike boy pupil was beginning to atrophy.

(*Pause*)
MISS MOFFATT: 'Ow you doin' boyo?
(*Pause*)
BOY: I'm OK, Miss.
(*Pause*)
MISS MOFFATT: How green is your valley then, bach?
(*Pause*)
BOY: It's OK, Miss.
(*Pause*)
MISS MOFFATT: How green is your corn then?
(*Pause*)
BOY: Pretty good, Miss. OK.
(*Huge pause*. Then angrily:)
MISS MOFFATT: Have you seen the *Squire* here or thereabouts or whereabouts then?
(*Pause*)

It suddenly hit me. Christ! I'm *off*! The Squire should have entered three and a half minutes ago for his *last scene*!

Hot with shame and now hearing a soft voice chanting, 'Mr Adams on stage please – you are *off* – Mr Adams,' I clattered down the metal ladder and hurtled through the set door like a whirling dervish and came to a halt on stage.

'Ah! Miss Moffat, I trust I find you well,' I puffed. 'Where have you been all this time?'

All Miss Moffatt could do was to scowl.

This was showbizniz, so we carried on.

Was my corn green?

Was my face red.

I apologised to Lionel and he said, 'Don't let it happen again, darling.'

I have an unfortunate predilection for 'being off' or missing my entrance in a play, and I suffer this syndrome gallantly whilst other actors suffer it less well.

It happened that I was 'off' yet again at the panto. Lionel was playing the Dame, as was the tradition, whilst I was depicting the fat monk Friar Tuck.

The panto always started half an hour earlier than usual, and as I checked in at the theatre with my bicycle the chief technician at the stage door said, 'Ah, you! They're looking for you.'

Then I heard the sound of the opening number, 'Oh the barnyard is busy in a regular tizzy, and the obvious reason is because of the season' over the tannoy.

Dismounting, I ricocheted back stage and was just in time to see Friar Tuck pass me in the corridor, looking very anorexic, eyes swimming with fear, grasping a tattered script and gibbering some lines to himself. The theatre board was in that night and apparently found the opening scene perplexing.

Minutes later, after changing into my padded costume with the speed of a red-arsed blowfly, I was pushed on to the stage. By this time the scene had changed; we had left the farmyard and were now in King John's castle. The courtiers, sundry servants, knights at arms, soldiers and the Miss Denise Pitt Draffen Dancing Academy pretended not to notice my stricken bulk frozen centre stage. After agonising seconds, displaying great presence of mind, I gathered up my monkish skirts and ran, hiding until my next scene.

At a convenient moment Lionel wandered over and murmured, in character, and in my ear: 'Don't let it happen again, darling.'

I was an 'Equity Deputy' at the Rep for some time – the official name for the 'loveys' shop steward. The seventies was heavily political and was therefore well versed in the art of analysing contractual verbiage and deciphering diatribes, facing the rigours of Corin Redgrave on a Monday morning and being asked to call a Union meeting there and then to ban Marius Goring from ever appearing in the West End again. This seemed to me to be as gross a piece of Bonapartism as ever I saw and I told the Workers' Revolutionary Party so and no messing.

Be that as it may, we were introduced one morning tea-break to a boyish, quiet, gentle man who was seconded to the Rep as a trainee director. He was empowered to direct a production of *Murder at the Vicarage* (by Agatha

Christie) and even tried to bring into it an element of Brecht, which didn't really work. One of our permanent actors, who had been at the Rep for some years, was furious with his small part in it and suggested, waspishly, that Equity should be approached with a view to our getting extra money for having to work with downright rank amateurs.

That amateur was soon to become Kenneth Loach.

The gimlet-eyed, seething and dynamic actress, Freda 'Woman of Twilight' Jackson – wife of Northampton pre-Raphaelite artist Henry Bird (who taught me chiaroscuro at the art school) – had been engaged to play Lady Bracknell in *The Importance of Being Earnest*.

Come Monday and the dress rehearsal, Miss Jackson announced that she would have to retire from the engagement as she was feeling stricken with the vapours. She swept into the wings and was *off*.

A ghastly hush pervaded the theatre.

It was eventually mooted that this was an emergency and that Lionel should play Lady Bracknell, willy nilly. That night the curtain rose and Lionel minced on in a ladylike manner, grasping the script, and proceeded to play the grand lady rather in the manner of the pantomime Dame. Forget gender, and quite right too. It all went downhill very well and the theatre zeitgeist ushered in similar avant garde productions of the classics in transvestite style, from the RSC and the National Theatre downwards.

I complimented Lionel on the original delivery of the line 'a hnHHANd-BBAGG!' and told him that I hoped it all wouldn't happen again.

Lionel's interpretation, originally delivered by Dame Edith Evans and recorded on phonograph, set a trend. But these three words now cry out for a new interpretation – new parameters – indeed – a new *sound*.

I have listed here some suggestions for investigating this (grey) area for an actor who wants a handle on to Wilde:

> A hand bag!
> Uhn'anbgg (mate)
> en hender begger (S Africa)
> ein hansbahg (German)
> a nan bag (Indian)
> una andio baggio (Italian)
> Uhr An Bog (Iceland)
> Ahaaaaoooooooooooont bag (Swiss)
> Ooh la la baguette (France)

Accents

There has long been contention among literary actors of the Classical School concerning the placing of the accent on certain words, particularly those that are to be found in the interstices of Shakespeare's text. A rehearsal can be brought to a halt when one comes across such a sentence as, say:

> 'My Lord, his skill upon the viol de gambois is consummate'
> 'My Lord, his skill upon the viol de gambois is con*summut*'
> 'My Lord, his skill upon the viol de gambois is consu*mmate*'

or:

> 'My Lord, I will per*severe* in my merry task'
> 'My Lord, I will per*sever* in my merry task'
> 'My Lord, I will just persevere'

Egos can inflate in the confines of a rehearsal room; truculent and pedantic actors may insist on 'Speaking the speech I pray you as *I* would have it spoken!' – mouthing the syllables that *they* deem correct to the annoyance of the speech coach who advises otherwise.

Make-up

The technical advances in stage lighting are now so sophisticated that there is no need for traditional make-up unless you are aged twenty-one and playing King Lear. As a youngster I noted that the faces of the actors were hand-coloured an unusually bright orange, coupled with what appeared to be red dots painted in the corner of the eye and bright blue around the eyelids. The crow's-feet lines of age in actresses were heavily painted over to deceive even the back row, with an effect like that of a masked ingénue from *Madame Butterfly*. The young gentlemen looked like Ivor Novello.

I kept my make-up requirements in a biscuit tin, a touching habit of the poorer player. Having not used it for many years, I thought I would have a peep at where it had been lying for all those years in the corner of the junk room at home.

It took several minutes to wrench the rusted lid off with a tin-opener. It was like meeting old friends again, which released in me memories and smells of yesteryear – *Murder At Key Cottage, All Girls Together, No Sex Please We're British*.

I began to examine the contents.

The vanishing cream had gone.

The nose putty had hardened into the shape of my last performance of Cyrano de Bergerac.

Lake – for red noses (alcoholic).

Here were sticks Nos 5 and 9 (pasty, creamy and earthy dark red).

A mini book of voice exercises. For example:

> 'MAH NAH LAH THAH VAR ZAH
> MAY NAY LAY THAY VAY ZAY
> MEE NEE LEE THEE VEE ZEE
> MAW NAW LAW THAW VAW ZAW
> MOO NOO LOO THOO VOO ZOO
> The sound is to be continuous, thus
> MOONOOLOOTHOOVOOZOO'

Also found was a rotting hare's foot and a desiccated tiny teddy bear.

Ah – there was that scaly, unhealthy looking green paste – I was playing Caliban in *The Tempest* at the time it was last used.

I once heard two cleaning ladies pass my dressing room during a matinee of *The Tempest* saying one to the other, 'That actor in there – oim so worried 'bout 'im – he looks *so* ill, don't he?'

What would they have made of my later triumph in *The Elephant Man*?

Poisonous metals can still play dangerous havoc in the tinsel-town theatre of today and bring it to its knees.

On the last night of *The Rocky Horror Show* our 'Rocky', naked except for an over-elaborate jockstrap and boots, suffered an invasion of silver glitter into the more vulnerable parts of the genitalia, causing this organ to blow up – or, shall we rather say, enlarge to monstrous phallic proportions. As he was suffering great pain, the show had to be cancelled. Luckily this was during a break in the run so 'Rocky' could recover in the arms of antibiotics.

Was it not Edmund Purdom who, suddenly, just before curtain-up, became aware that he had lost his black socks for a dinner party scene with which the play opened?

Like a true 'pro' he quickly painted his ankles with black greasepaint.

With the Royals

I am not a Monarchist but I have enjoyed proximity with Royalty, even cronied with them, although I can only dream of Mustique. Princess Margaret graced us with her presence at the Wimbledon Theatre for the Actors' Company's performance of *Widowers' Houses* (Bernard Shaw), a play about slum landlords. When the curtain came down we lined up on stage behind it and the Princess weaved and wandered her way down the line, smiling. When she reached me, she stopped, seemingly a little tongue-tied, so I embarked on a little homily about homelessness not having changed much in this day and age. Her eyes went glassy. Within seconds she had moved smoothly down the line and disappeared up her exit.

This was either an unwillingness to argue a point, or just bad breath.

Tod

Actors and agents often suffer a disturbed relationship – the actor accusing the agent of 'being lazy and not doing anything for me' and the agent accusing the actor of 'being lazy and not doing anything for me'.

My agent, Tod Joseph, of Joseph and Wagg (I never found out who Wagg was), owned me for thirty years and we always had a cross word for one another whenever we could. Over the years I still kept him down to 10% commission (for commercials as well), when a lot of other actors were being charged 15% and rising.

I escaped from Tod only once. I felt, after several years' bonding, that Tod was 'being lazy and not doing anything for me' so I thought I'd test the waters of oblivion and send some private begging letters to other agents – under plain cover. Within the hour I had been found out. I didn't realise how closely agents were in each other's pockets. Literally.

I was summonsed to Mr Joseph's office in Bond Street where I found him in tears.

'Watcha do this to me for? What have I done to you?' he moaned. 'I never thought you'd do this to me. Ingrate!' Whereupon he seized an eighteenth-century horsewhip that was leaning by the fireplace and gave me a sharp, vituperative flick on the left buttock. I bit back my tears. (Tod was a collector of antiques.)

Pulling himself together, he said, 'I will not increase your commission to 10½% and you'll go before Equity *and* the PMA. By the way, Frinton has offered you *Macbeth*. You'd better go home and think about it. And if you *do* do it – don't forget – 10½%!'

I gave a short intake of breath.

A unique service provided by Tod was the cryptic postscripts scrawled at the bottom of one's financial statements – they show something of Tod's sometimes rather low humour, eg:

'The enclosed will just about pay for the first course at Rules next Saturday. Sorry to hear you're down to your last thousand dollars, lovey.'

'Like Lazarus, I rose from my bed especially to relieve myself of your anal hoard; I have no wish, sirrah, to go through such motions again. Get my drift?'

'Don't invest it all at once – keep some for the taxman wot cometh – you capitalist swine you, or the Vat is in the fire. Shall I bring a Securicor van? Sincere regards, Tod.'

'Just think! 52 weeks hard cheese in *The Mouse Crap* at £300 per week – the best offer yet. How d'ye fancy a year's shirk? NOTALOT. Wilkommen, Tod.'

'You're going to have to make the lolly last, as I go to Shrublands Health Farm for a fortnight on Saturday to lose "pounds" – in more senses of the word than one, and Debbie is not very proficient on the abacus. Sincere regards – Tod.'

And some days later:

> 'Still down here at Skull Thumpers Hall – now in my second week of my fortnightly fight against the flab.
> The intake last week was not too geriatric; the resident mortician not having too much difficulty in judging the quick from the dead. However, among the current lot, there are one or two real old trouts.
> Keep off the grass – don't fall on your arse.
> Ecce homo – go home, uomo and stay der.
> Sincere regards – Creejus Josephuis.'

Tod moved office and flat to Brixton and enjoyed the atmosphere there until his flat and office were broken into by two youths who robbed him after tying him up. Some weeks later he heard what emerged to be the same robbers again attempting to break in. He was able to call the police, who thwarted them.

From this time on Tod was a haunted, fearful man. It was not long before he died. It has been suggested that his illness was the result of his terrifying experiences.

He could be irascible and rude, but we celebrated his life at the Actors' Church, Covent Garden.

He had integrity, loyalty and compassion.

When I heard over the telephone of Tod's death, I sat down on the stairs and cried.

Rocky Horror

Many years ago, Tod, my agent, telephoned me and said I should go along to an audition at the Royal Court Theatre that afternoon.

'Downstairs?'

'Upstairs.'

'That gloomy room?'

'Yep.'

'Why? Am I going to do *Macbeth* at Frinton after all?'

'Oh, shut up! I've got a lot of work to catch up on.'

'What's it all about then?'

'Sounds a bit indulgent to me – in it there is a body-builder, a creature from outer space, an all-American couple, a mad professor – suit you…'

'Shudup!'

'…a rock'n'roll biker, a transvestite…'

'OK! I'll go. What time? Who do I talk to?'

'Richard O'Brien or Jim Sharman.'

'Never heard of them…'

Mr O'Brien was an engaging, pleasant person, with a touch of the Mephisto Waltz about him. Looking then much as he does today – sporting long, dark tresses, as was the fashion in those halcyon days of *Hair*, but now given to complete wilful baldness, exposing one of Mother Nature's more sensitively modelled craniums, one that, indeed, could have come from a Red Dwarf. His 'turn out', different every day, was still a faint shock – the thin whiplash-taut body and sparkling costume. He has long been a master of Pulp Parody.

Jim Sharman, the quiet director, wore shoes with huge high heels and also wore his hair long. He was something of an enfant terrible in Australia where he had massacred Mozart opera from time to time. I was to join them again after *Rocky Horror* in a play by Sam Shepherd, again at the Court, with Mike Pratt.

I auditioned for 'Rocky' by performing a little operatic parody I had written, 'Heybahbahblack Sheep'.

They found it rather cute. I landed the role.

My part was that of a narrator, a sepulchral moralist who observes and comments darkly on the corrupt antics of the louche figures that cavort before him. The part wasn't of much consequence at first, but built up as we rehearsed. An image was beginning to evolve – at £18 per week – in the drab room called 'The Theatre Upstairs'. A steeply raked catwalk spliced the acting space in two, tilting into the auditorium the unseemly characters as they made their entrances.

That opening night in 'The Theatre Upstairs' in 1972 will be remembered for Tim Curry, the quiet son of a Methodist chaplain, as he strode ferociously down the perilous walkway on his high heels to a blast of rock music and his own vibrant voice, displaying what has since become an established archetypal image for kitsch lovers. A howl of glee and whelping whoops of delight shook the tiny theatre.

It was a hit!! Every night!

Thirty years later, the show still totters on, in tights, to this very day.

And so…

'I would like, if I may, to take you on a strange journey…'

As I sit in my threadbare, tartan dressing gown (I no longer dress in dark velvet for dinner after a show) relaxing in 'Tomb View', where my grounds abut the St Pancras and Islington Cemetery, warming my cracked lips on the bone china 'Rocky' memento mori mug, full of hot stirred cocoa …

…Oh! And … here comes again the 'Passing Parade' – a multitude of artists who have travelled along the Rocky path on their astounding journeys to perdition, these creatures of the night.

I had long put away, into my fancy-dress drawer, my fishnet tights and suspenders – I never did feel they were quite me – when suddenly the cosmic mode changed.

At last! *The Rocky Horror Picture Show.*

The movie was out.

Some were in, some were out. I was in.

The sinister Mr Charles Gray, a new arrival ('some chicken, no neck'), slid into my old role of Narrator – now known in the USA as 'The Criminologist' – and I became Doctor (Scotty) Scott, the Weird Professor in the wheelchair who eventually discloses his very fine legs in fishnet tights, which Gillian Lynne was to appreciate some years later.

I was glad of this change-over because Mr Gray had only one or so days' filming and then disappeared into television and I filmed for six weeks, thus receiving more money than he. I needed the money more than he did – I had had a Marital Bust-Up.

A new format established itself.

The audience took to the habit of shouting out personal remarks in unison to the actors in the film, who weren't listening.

Mr Gray suffered the question, 'Where's your fuggin' neck??' This nightly abuse went over his head. My part was just greeted with the simple statement 'BORING!'. No matter – I wasn't there either.

The movie girded itself up then spun off at a tangent to movie houses all over the world.

It became a shrine for tout le monde.

With my golden disc, celebrating half a million record sales of 'Rocky', hanging above my steaming bath, I now know I can sleep soundly because I am, quite frankly, a cult.

The film, as I interpret it, is a ritual in which the audience participates. What appears to be a secular quasi-religious pantomime now takes place during every screening.

The bizarre characters conjured up by Mr O'Brien are still dancing past me and I am again in a glossy laboratory with the sexually mysterious Frank N. Furter.

Pat Quinn (now called M'lady Patricia) occasionally returns to slum a little, selling ice-cream from her tray. Tell me, is Michael Rennie still ill or was it indigestion? Tim hides himself whenever he can. Little Nell tip-taps round East 41 block as kooky as ever. Is Meat Loaf now a vegetarian? Certainly Sarandon is a STAR in 'HOLLYWOOD'. Richard doesn't look well. Must we do the Time Warp AGAIN?

Rocky himself seems to have disappeared in the fuss – an enigmatic creature of the night. He must have worked on his torso and muscularity for years to get the role.

The show has become almost fundamentalist to its devotees. Several rituals are enacted, ie the lighting of candles en masse and the throwing of rice.

The chanting of an evolving text which is either silly, or obscene, or both, is regularly practised and a new role-model of fan has arisen that goes berserk whilst dressed in the character of its choice.

These fans imitate the cast's costumes and make-up with obsessional precision.

Soon on the scene a benign character called Sal Piro emerged as a young Rocky High Priest for the fans, and the idea of holding a 'Convention' blossomed. Sal, something of a comedian, had seen the film one thousand and two times 'and that's for starters, Scotty.'

A fan club having been formed, two of the keenest enthusiasts, John Mandrachia and his friend Paul, arranged with Piro to launch this 'Rocky Horror Convention' in New York, where, for a small sum, the real cast would flounce before the cameras or sing 'The Time Warp'.

When Pat Quinn and I arrived in New York, to be met by John Mandrachia and Paul, we were amazed to meet what appeared to be two *schoolboys* who greeted us with, 'Hi, baby,' and 'Hi, baby,' before pushing us into a huge, stretch limo that was being surrounded by a growing crowd.

Inside this capsule was a whole new world of fancy dress having a party (now called 'partying'). A film of *The Wizard of Oz* was playing, music was rocking and wine and beer were flowing ('Yuh c'n have as much beer as yuh c'n drink, Jonathan'), and tequila was being offered all round. It seemed to create a sensation of being in the bowl of an aquarium whilst observing the outer world being played out as a mime. Disconcerting globular faces goggled at us through the windows. Delirium!

We were sped to the Algonquin Hotel to wash up and brush down and for thieves to relieve Mizz Quinn of all her money and means of living.

On arrival I was asked if I would be wanting to try on a panty girdle and high heels. I gracefully declined.

That night Pat and I were whipped round at high speed to four cinemas spilling out 'Rocky' all over New York. We were announced as visiting stars and shown off. Each time the audience howled. The guarding and guiding boys clung to us protectively in the theatrical manner of minders through the heavily sweating fans seeking autographs.

Towards 3am we were still there.

The Convention

This was to be launched the next day and was staged in a vast two-thousand-seater dance hall. It was to be the first of several such manifestations – the whole ROCKYMANIA – free gifts for the lucky ones, a competition for the best costume, our LIVE ON STAGE numbers, performances by the most accomplished 'look-alikes', a floor show and the dispensation of rice. The climax came with the sudden illumination by candlelight – all very American!

Come the final hours to pay up, before the performance, there appeared two sinister gentlemen, having the aura of mafiosi, who were financing the extravaganza. We began to ask when our pitifully small fees were to be paid.

Forestalling, they smiled at us and regretted that we must wait a few hours more, perhaps until after the show – 'Don't worry, baby'. I said that we would like to have it *now* as per contract.

Little Nell, who is no slouch, shrieked, 'If we don't get the money by midday then – *no show*!'

I observed the demeanour of these gentlemen who were obviously taken aback by being talked tough to by a kooky *woman*.

The dimes were duly handed over and the convention convened.

My father

During the run of the stage version of *Rocky Horror* my father died, aged eighty-six. He always tried to follow the shows I was playing in.

During my three years at Northampton Rep he was regularly to be found sitting in the stalls, row F, on every second night of the first week of the run. Perhaps it was 'all for the best' that he never saw 'Rocky'. It would not have been his 'cup of tea'.

His puritanism, though, was not perhaps any more or less different from that of his Edwardian generation. My father still had a disturbed emotional residue from being incarcerated in his prison camp for three and a half years in the Great War. My mother once remarked that his behaviour could be eccentric; he jealously followed her at one time.

He had a concept of 'normality' or 'weak-mindedness' and was judgemental with a fear of the extravagance of the 'dark wells of the subconscious'. I hear that the subconscious is rather out of date now in the new world of the cognitive.

In spite of inhibitions, he was an interesting father when not bowed down by worry. He would tell tales of the Great War, study lepidoptera, the possibility of taking up yachting on the Broads, the craft of etching (aforementioned), designing his garden, painting and drawing, plus photography. His favourite writer was H. G. Wells.

As he grew older we became closer and in later years we developed a rapport. My brother and I helped him along. Then he began to weaken and we moved his furniture down to my marital home in 'Tomb View', but within that week he died. I was appearing in the theatre every night while he was in hospital and then he began to die. Under the old adage 'The show must go on' I still feel sad that I missed his actual death while I continued to play that night. I feel guilty about that; an understudy could have taken over for that night.

He was a man who had both humour and compassion.

Actors' Company

I've never missed a day off work (in showbizniz) with the exception of the time when I suffered a broken nose in Curitiba (Brazil).

It all began with the Actors' Company, the bright vision of Ian McKellen and Edward Petherbridge. The watchword was Democracy and a commitment to tour Britain (and, as it happened, the world).

The actors became the management.

The management became the actors. I sometimes say 'actresses' for 'actors' as was traditional and lucid.

We enjoyed endless meetings when we voted for this and for that. (Enjoyed?)

What plays should we mount?

The British Council suggests the following (they are putting up the money):

Scenario:
Plug Britain's grandeur (as was).
Check out theatres abroad, if any, for possible workable venues in what's
  left of the British Empire: (Theme)
The Bahamas, Bermuda, Cayman Islands, Montserrat, St Helena,
  Ascension, Gibraltar, Turks & Caicos, Grenada, Lundy Island.
What plays? George Bernard Shaw, Pinter and Coward's *Cavalcade*
  ('Sshum mishtake, shawley? Where do we find hundreds of extras?')
Tour Great Britain: start with Billingham. Get that over with.
What actors to engage.
What actresses to engage.
Gielgud? Scofield? Blessed? (Too expensive. Would they want to?)
Would *you* tour for £70 per week? (I did.)
Will they be democratically minded?
Good company members?
Casting ourselves. (Tricky)
We vote for those company members who submit themselves for the next
  tour.
Each contestant exits with a wry laugh (defensive) whilst voting takes place.
Each contestant asked back into room. ('What's the damage?')
There may be tears... There were tears.

To be the wrong side of casting is a unique experience not granted to most actors. The actor's depravities and/or great talents are idly bandied about:

Too old? Too young? Too smart?
Too much of the (you know), the hard stuff.

I adored him!
STUNNING!
USELESS!
GORGEOUS!
A pain in the neck!
Sally? Too, too doolally.
She's very bizarre, don't you think?
A good, solid performer, I think.
If he gets the part it's a recipe for disaster, darling.
If he comes – I'm off.
All members are expected to understudy.
All members are expected to play small parts (big as well).
All members are expected to play big parts (and small) and so…

I was bemused when we had our first meeting of the new company in the empty bar of the Wimbledon Theatre (the company's 'home') to see the most elderly actor, after listening for ten minutes, begin, very slowly, to slither smoothly down behind the back of the bar and disappear from sight with a slight thump. An awareness of this grew upon the gathered company until all were silenced. Then there came the sound of light snoring.

I don't think I ever saw him at a meeting again.

I was lucky enough to get voted in for the Foreign Tour – my old granny used to say, 'A pretty face can get you anywhere!' I was cast playing a country man and a rent collector with three months in Jamaica, Mexico, Brazil and Argentina.

You will read here that I will be left in Brazil for reasons to be explained in a minute.

The tour was a cornucopia of cocktails every evening after the show – meeting with local dignitaries in situ, grandees, panjandrums, Ministers, Trustees, Consuls, Cultural Attachés and Ambassadors – the Beau Monde…

I enjoyed the British Council swimming pool and the exquisite canapes.

In the grounds of Jamaica House the girls ordered a rum drink called 'White Witch'. The waitress served them sourly muttering, 'White Witch? White shit!'

The feeling gradually dawned that one was not wanted.

As we left she shrieked, 'White Bitch, man!'

However, it must be said that, every night, the audiences were invariably superb.

In Mexico *The Rocky Horror Show* was playing next door – a pirated version, Richard O'Brien told me later. We were also playing (according to the poster) Ayckbourn's *How the Other Hoves Lives* (sic), very successfully (I was not in that one). Nearby was that famous singer, billed as 'Victoria from Los Angeles'. We took in the mighty Aztec ruins and more – marvellous cathedrals to boot. All a bit of a rush!

It was time to go on to Brazil and we had planned to have an important meeting whilst on the long flight from Mexico to Curitiba in Brazil (no rest). But as we couldn't resist looking out of the windows to see the endless ranges of the Andes, which stirred us greatly, we jettisoned the plans for the meeting and gave ourselves over to the mighty unfolding of Nature. Do it mañana.

There seemed to be a lot of jungle left…

Curitiba is a university town some way in from the others we would be visiting. We unpacked there – it was a 'cool' town – after which we were to perform in Brasilia, Rio and Sao Paulo.

In Curitiba we had arranged to attend a party after the show and were being driven the right way by a girl who was connected with the Council. Suddenly, we were being driven the wrong way, eg up the wrong way of what was the right way in a one-way thoroughfare.

We smashed into another car. My head catapulted forward and hit the car's front window. Barbara Murray's jaw was broken. No one was wearing seat belts, if such existed. The driver, costumier and Stage Manager were relatively unscathed.

Gradually I became aware that I was sitting in a hospital, in the middle of the night, gibbering repetitive gibberish, à la dada, which seemed to be coming from a long way away. Outside was the hectic hustle and bustle of hospitals. It seemed that by now most of the company had been sent back to the hotel. The British Council gentleman was wandering around perplexed. Barbara Murray was looking shocked in a corner. She was sent home to England the next day.

I was sent back to the hotel where I could see the others. I became aware that I had a broken nose.

Daylight fell. Stephanie Turner took over Barbara's part but poor Simon Cadell, very nervously, took over my part the next night with the aid of a script. Luckily, the play that night was the Pinter and this contained plenty of long pauses during which Simon could reflect on the next line.

Urgent meetings tried to solve the immediate problems of keeping the show going. I was sent to hospital to de-flatten my nose. This was corrected and I went back to my old part of the rent collector.

Then my nose again began to bleed, unstoppably this time, during the show. It was back to the hospital; my nose was stuffed with a kind of sausage of wadding that started at the nose and ended emerging from the mouth. Very claustrophobic. I began to wake during the operation and listened to incomprehensible jolly Portuguese chatting.

The company pushed on, leaving me in Curitiba with a bandaged head and sunglasses, looking like the Invisible Man. Somehow the company managed to survive the rest of the tour without my artistic contribution.

I was sent off to convalesce in Sau Paulo and Rio de Janeiro and enjoyed the hospitality of the British Council gentlemen and their lady wives.

I never saw Argentina. Although I later performed the 'Masochism Tango' in the show *Tomfoolery*, I never learned how to execute a genuine tango in Argentina and frighten Gillian Lynne, which would have been useful for the dancing career I was thinking of building back in Blighty.

Eventually, I had my bandages removed and the nose was still there, in situ, and appeared to be the remembered standard shape. Or was it?

Every time I passed a mirror I couldn't help stopping and looking at my nose and debating with myself about its flexibility. One day it seemed like Rembrandt's nose, another day it was getting bigger and bigger like Pinocchio or even Pulchinella.

Having faith in my potential, I began to cast my line by writing letters to all the theatrical producers in Britain suggesting that I ought to be considered for a new production of 'Bergerac' as my nose was growing more purpose-built by the day. I had already played in *Bergerac* with John Nettles for the television series as a pathologist in a morgue, but this pretty kettle of fish was a whole new ball game. As you see, I was a little confused after the accident. It had disturbed my brains more than I thought. I was recommended some good brain surgeons in Rio.

Wasn't there a character called 'Cyrano' in it?

Fumms Bo Wah ta zaooo.

Pogiff.

Master Class

List of characters:
Stalin
Prokofiev
Shostakovich
Zhdanov
Playwright: David Pownall
Director: Justin Green

No historical personage is free from the literary trawl of the above-mentioned playwright and I had the honour of appearing in two of his plays – a radio work in which I played a 'Yeltzin' who didn't quite make it on to the tarmac when he arrived in Dublin to meet the Irish Prime Minister – and in *Master Class* at the Leicester Haymarket, the Old Vic and Wyndhams.

Zhdanov (me), a commissar, and Stalin (Timothy West) spend a terrifying, but funny night in the Kremlin where we engage in an uproarious critical dialectic with Prokofiev (Peter Kelly) and Shostakovich (David Bamber).

Among the various Russian exiles visiting the show – Prokofiev's son and mother among them – was the conductor Rudolf Barshai. He had played at the funerals of Stalin and Prokofiev, both of these passing thither on the same day. Barshai was invited on to the stage before the show to be introduced to us. Because of time, we were already made up. Barshai came in through the wings, saw Timothy West in his Stalin frock and stopped in his tracks. He confessed to having had quite a shock, as if Uncle Joe had risen from the dead and had come to haunt him.

Unfortunately, on another night, Tim West's moustache became restive and, because spirit gum holds such an enmity with perspiration that it will not adhere, he peeled it off and dumped it in a samovar. This is the kind of thing an audience loves. Transfer this happening in Russia in the forties and Tim, besides losing his moustache, would have lost both his Equity Card and freedom, in the Gulag.

Tomfoolery

In 1980 Gillian Lynne, dynamo choreographer, took four of us actors under her tutu and, under the further aegis of Cameron Mackintosh, as he was then before he launched that feline bombshell, *Cats*. (And the rest is mystery. Did they actually make a musical based on the poetry of *T. S. Eliot*? Who else?)

Brian Blessed can confirm this as he was in it.

Gillian choreographed us four in *Tomfoolery*, a revival of the satirical songs of Tom Lehrer. We were Robin Ray – that doyen of musical quizzes and panel games – Martin Connor, Patricia George and me. It was an exciting challenge to revive the songs of Tom Lehrer. Tom Lehrer? Was he that singer who was also a mathematics professor at Harvard? Surely he was dead? He had long stopped rasping out those scabrous songs that sounded like a corncrake croaking and made him famous in the fifties. He had gone back to studying numbers but now he was out to revive himself at the Criterion Theatre.

Our revival showed that the subject matter was still as pungent and relevant in 1980 as it was in the fifties: the atom bomb – pigeon droppings – dope-peddling – the Vatican – boy scouts – animal husbandry – assorted American phenomena… We will all go together when we go…

I performed a number dealing with 'smut' in which I paraded a bowler-hatted, pin-stripe-suited type, sporting an umbrella. Gillian directed the show as elaborately as ever and almost made a walkdown number of my 'smut'. She had me twirl and move my umbrella in a highly dextrous and dangerous manner, rather in the style of Astaire.

Not being one of Britain's top dancers, I found it difficult to grapple with this umbrella and not appear wholly gauche. At the end of each day I would be apprehended whilst trying to escape through the back door and Miss Lynne would call imperiously for the umbrella to be brought in – sharpish – like an instrument of torture and I was again forced to go through my paces like a horse in a circus. Eventually, after having achieved some sort of rapport with the umbrella, I dropped it one night during the show.

There was a deathly silence. It had to happen.

Miss Lynne was in the country and was planning to cast me in a balletic version of the opera *Wozzeck* in which I would play the Drum Major. The idea was gently dropped, as was the baton.

Later in the run, besides being attacked by a 'nervous complaint', I began to feel sharp twinges in my groin. This was soon diagnosed as an old-fashioned inguinal hernia, the curse of the working dancer.

It was obvious that Miss Lynne's taut, tight, mean choreography with its demonic entrechats and fois de gris point neuf work had wrecked my movement muscles and it was plain that my future as a dancer at Sadlers Wells was finished.

It is worth noting that during rehearsals, Miss Lynne expressed pleasure at the shape of my legs, which I return.

Tom Lehrer sent a card for the first night of *Tomfoolery*, which I resisted including in the book, but then I couldn't resist it… Lovely man…

Dear Jonathan –
Now that it's too late to turn back, I wanted to write a brief fan letter to thank you for all that your unique and delightful comic talents have brought to the show. I cannot overestimate your versatility, which has brought out things in the songs that even I hadn't realized were there. It has been a pleasure watching your demonstrations of gentle insanity, and I shall miss seeing you perform. Best of luck to you, both in this show and in the future.
With gratitude and affection,
Tom

Dr Johnson

A character I enjoyed playing at the Edinburgh Traverse and The Royal Court theatres was Dr Johnson. The play was *Heaven and Hell* by Dusty Hughes (no relation to a Miss Springfield) and was directed by Richard Wilson.

Richard is a very funny actor. At rehearsals he found delight in throwing bags, full of what I took to be beans, at us actors and giggling as they thwapptt us across the chops – an old Gaelic custom pertaining to the Scottish theatre, I understand, designed to break us down and encourage love for one another in theatrical empathy.

It is said that acting in the theatre is a technical exercise creating illusion. Yet others will say it is an outpouring of the soul from its very depths that must be experienced nightly by the actor.

My entrance as the great Doctor was backed by the unearthly strains of Albinoni. I had to lumber forth and sit down centre forward on a rickety chair looking very sad indeed but not saying anything. Apparently he was a gloomy beggar.

At rehearsals I became aware that a certain musical note, in despairing minor key, was of such melancholy that, willy-nilly, it would always trigger off a genuine, unstoppable tear. I found I could not resist repeating this particular sob without fail when I heard the note, no matter how I was feeling. During performances, the Pavlovian emotion released by this tear duct increased every night until the audience would bring out handkerchiefs.

Michael Billington, the theatre critic, thought it was the most profound moment of the production.

As the run continued, I became enslaved by my musical sensitivity. Emotionally I couldn't help moving myself every night and indulged in narcissistic reverie. Time pitched forward and was of no concern as I waited for that haunting note and its aftermath every evening.

It came to a head when I was so moved by my own performance that I sat there, pleasantly pole-axed, sobbing softly.

The music had finished when the prompter whispered, 'Mr Adams, please clear the stage for the next scene. Now!'

Bemused, I became aware of stage hands hurriedly moving furniture and props around me.

I had to be led from the stage. I had snapped.

Technicality or Emotionalism? Which was it?

Stanislavsky might have had a word for it. But I don't know which one.

Metropolis

In 1992 entrepreneur Michael ('Rocky') White mounted a production of *Metropolis* at the Piccadilly Theatre. Book by Joe Brooks and inspired by Fritz Lang's silent classic movie, the story takes place in a futuristic mechanised world where the workers have become mute slaves, except when they sing a number. Unrest is quelled by the persuasion of a saintly girl, Maria, but a weirdo inventor creates a 'doppelganger' to incite them to revolt. On top of all this is a love story (played out by Graham Bickley and Judy Kuhn).

A superb set of the subterranean city was designed by Rolf Koltai. The audience left the theatre 'humming' it. There was little else to hum. I played the professor who had invented the city, and Brian Blessed, once of *Z Cars* fame, was the Big Boss.

The production did not run smoothly; factions fought furiously; Brian was having trouble, so I tried to help him. He would visit me before curtain-up for spiritual advice and we had many a powerful and thought-provoking converzazione.

I developed an increasing admiration for the mighty range of Brian's vocabulary. He would hail me with fond names like 'Pillock', 'Prat', 'Bollock-Face' and, not to put too fine a point in it, 'Arsehole'. He acknowledged a flattering admiration for my plainsong – and suggested that I should approach the management of *Brigadoon*, which was then playing in the West End, for a role in a kilt, but I thought it only fair to leave such openings to the lissom young dancers in our midst.

In return I suggested he should get himself a good singing teacher and apply for the next Joe Brooks-buster mediocre, muddled-message, multi-mega-musical, which would be opening soon at the Soho Poly and which we playfully suggested could be called *The Sound of Blessed*. 'Climb Every Mountain' should be done as a walkdown number with Blessed accompanied by his own tackle, rope-ladder, iron rations, swear box and Holy Bible, and furthermore, when in the middle of a rehearsal, it was suggested that he avoid suddenly leaving the stage with a crisp epithet before disappearing into the night for several days.

It was at these rehearsals of *Metropolis* that I was deeply stirred by this eye-popping musical's writhing birth-pangs – an intrepid band of hack horn and glockenspiel players, wrestling with a score that teetered at a tangent from *The Rite of Spring* and *The Great Gate of Kiev* to *I've Gotta Lovely Bunch of Coconuts*, and by a sweating troupe of mummers, fighting with a text that seemed almost Becket-like in its ramblings – wrestling sometimes with each other, in a rather saucy way, I often thought.

Here was creative democracy at work – actors queueing up every morning for a coffee and a piece of script for breakfast crying, 'Tell us, tell us, what is it *about*? And what part am I playing this morning, duckie?'

The Peter Brook avant garde was looking positively derrière. I still see in my mind's eye Mr Koltai's Meccano set, which I can only describe as a dangerous self-indulgence, dwarfing as it did the entire ensemble as they hustled bleeding from gangways, concussing their craniums on cog-wheels, slipping down lift shafts and disappearing down tubes and tunnels, fighting each day just to stay alive! It was only by a narrow squeak that I held on to my health every night during the run.

One of my scenes was set in my laboratory where I was about to perform surgery on a drugged Miss Kuhn, spread-eagled on an operating table, and just sing at her. All this was set on a small platform suspended by wires that were, hopefully, fixed to the ceiling. I had to clamber up ladders into the cavernous heights of the Piccadilly Theatre, mount the platform and start singing before facing the vertiginous journey down. If I looked below me I went green. I was told this mechanism didn't always perform correctly. There was a very real danger that it might jam up and the platform stick halfway down so that we might be stranded, say, five feet above the stage, still singing whilst the audience would begin to titter and the safety curtain, blessedly, rushed down. Time for an impromptu tea break while the stage staff got to work.

On a particularly ghastly night, one of the coiled wires suspending the platform snapped with a vicious twang, proceeding to coil on a wild trajectory as the platform began to pick up speed on its long journey down towards terra firma. Like a good 'pro', I continued singing my song as if nothing had happened (they don't make 'em like this any more). The taut audience was hushed and I could see the cast gathering in the wings to watch our impending deaths whilst the tannoy called the stage management crew to report to the prompt side immediately.

After what seemed like minutes, we hit the stage with a dull crash. The song had come to an end long before. Judy Kuhn was wondering what was happening and was helped off, whilst I, still on the platform (as plotted), started going up again. I could have dismounted, but I stayed for the journey back to the ceiling exit. On reflection, I was reminded of that old picture 'Faithful Unto Death' in which a Roman centurion 'carries on' as the ruins of a burning Pompeii melt around him.

One of the cast remarked, 'That ol' devil – he don' give a damn if we don' survive.'

'But we will survive!
Brightly alive!
Flying high!
Oh, me
Oh, my!'

The entire proceedings were conducted by an Impresario of Gallic extraction, a Monsieur Jerome Savory, who enjoined me to permit him to call me 'Mr Ross Biff' while I addressed him as 'M'sieur Savoir Faire'. Sartorially, he made a diminutive but striking figure, sporting a long, bright, conspicuously red scarf against the cold.

I learned from him that he had directed one hundred and one operas all over the world and that our young producer, Mike White, was a cheeky monkey to inform him that he had a little way to go as regards professionalism. Things were beginning to turn sour.

Mr Savory is also apparently famous as a bare-backed tiger trainer in an act he calls the 'Grand Magic Circus', and, coming from this rather vulgar background, wields a rawhide whip when on the continent, which he lays about him during blocking.

This procedure was quickly stamped on as being at odds with the British Equity contract.

One day, during final rehearsals, a day on which Jerome was absent, having fled to Paris for the night, fearing attack, I nipped out and into 'Dunkin Doughnuts', a burger den outside the theatre, to purchase a jammy pastry.

On my return, still masticating, I attempted to effect an entrance into the theatre and imagine my surprise when several burly security guards leapt upon me, tearing from my neck the long, bright, conspicuously red scarf I happened to be wearing, with savage cries of 'Gotcha mate! You fuckin' fat frog!'

Suddenly, I knew I had to get back into the theatre, quickly, to only-connect with Fritz Lang's zeitgeist. And *now*!

I rejoined that there must be some mistake as M'sieur Savory was away. It was only on the personal intervention of a retired tap dancer from the company that I was eventually released from their Rambo-like grip. I later learned that these security precautions had been taken by Mr Brook's many lawyers because it had become known that a death squad was on its way from Paris; I was warned to keep out of the way. I disappeared into my dressing room and immediately took out an insurance policy, booking myself into a room at the Denville Hall Home for Retired Thespians.

I was getting steamed up emotionally about this show and I needed another man-size doughnut to get me right on track again. I munched and munched again, discomforted by the bright red jam as it wilfully squirted, dunkin'-wise, down my front. Was I losing control?

Already pre-first-nighters were gathering, carrying sleeping bags. And me? Might I hit town?

Exhausted by now, I went back to my dressing room slumped on the dual-purpose casting couch and fell asleep.

Immediately I was jolted awake by the sound of an altercation. My dressing room was next to the stage door. I pricked up my ears:

'Zut alors! Merde alors!' (etc, etc, etc)

It was Mr Savory.

'But, Mr Savory…'

I was hearing the raised tones of the Company Manager…

'Please, Mr Savory…'

'Zis iz absoord!'

'Mr Savory, I have been instructed by the management not to allow you into the theatre and…'

'You can tell zis M'sieur Blanc zat I am LE DIRECTEUR EXTRAORDINAIRE of zis production… JE SUIS LE MAITRE!'

'Mr Savory, you must…'

'You zay zat I make merde of zis text? OK? OK? OK? Well gimmee a brook – I mean, gimmee a book, man – jus' gimme a FOIGINE BUUUCK!!!'

It was Jerome himself who informed me that musicals are targeted at people with a mental age of twelve; after that, I felt more comfortable. As we later saw, this target was realised, which, perhaps, explains the libretto where words are pared down to an almost rudimentary vocabulary. One may ponder the enigma of such lines as:

'1011011011011011011' etc (this line was written by writer Dusty Hughes, who was coerced into work on this musical late in rehearsals).

She's a witch, she's a witch, she's a witch, she's a witch, she's a witch, she's a witch, which witch is the witch?'

For the sun never shines 'cos I'm agoin' round the bend.'

'You are beau-ti-ful – X-kwisitt – but she must be destroyed.'

'She's a born alligator, but believe me, I'm touched by your elephants' (Brian was really on a roll here).

I would often meditate upon this text as I lingered in my dressing room in a state of reverie, listening to lovely Miss Bell (ASM) delivering her carefully coded messages over the tannoy:

'Good evening, ladies and gentlemen. Owing to indisposition Martin Knight will cover Bo Light, Mr Light will sing "Bring down my tights" and will cover up Stephen Colley; Graham Bickley will play Tom Eastwood who will stand in for Brian Blessed, Paul Koon Simon Shetton and Ann Shetton Lucy Barker is on for Jason Barker Christian Solari and MaHiri Vari will play Mata Hari Joseph Scott Lloyd will sing "Bring down the curtain and let's all go home".'

As they say, the show must go on. And on…

So I say farewell to the boys and girls of *Metropolis*. If any of you are reading this, bless you.

Farewell to Joe Brooks who is going back to the mid-West wheatfields to husk the corn. You light up my life, Joe, and I just can't put out the blaze.

'And don't forget…'(as Joe would say, with his satrap, Dusty Hughes, and a cheery wave from M'sieur Blanc):

> '…if once in a while
> you catch yourself crying:
> If you're a little sad
> You'll know – it wasn't so bad
> When the show had to come off:
> Our dear, dear 'Metropolis'
> Goodnight
> The Party's over
> Hava hava hava hava
> Have a nice day.'

So pack up your make-up and LET'S GET THIS SHOW *OFF* THE ROAD!'

Epilogue

Now I never knew that a certain Doc Parky had introduced himself insidiously some way back in the Passing Parade – a gentleman who takes his time – a veritable procrastinator that gradually makes himself felt. He arrives quietly and gate-crashes very subtly.

I have some slight compensation though – when addressing me, talk to me with respect, for I was once a cult. Thank you.

'Balancing act'

Postscript

The 'Dr Parky' gently referred to by Jonathan at the end of his book was Parkinson's disease. He was finally diagnosed with this illness just as he had completed the book in 1997. He died on 13th June 2005 after suffering for eight years the frustrations and indignities of the disease in his wonderfully uncomplaining and tolerant fashion.

When Jonathan was young he already had signs of depression, which continued throughout his life but which he covered up in public with his sharp, but never unkind, wit, causing everyone else to laugh whilst being unable to himself. His po-faced humour was brilliantly exposed in his one-man shows where he accompanied his own outrageously funny songs at the piano.

Jonathan's depression and nightmarish dreams may have been the reason why, whilst studying art in his youth, he took great interest in the Dadaist movement that preceded Surrealism. He moved on to Surrealism, which remained with him to the end, many of his best works being surreal collages.

He was an intrepid traveller, enjoying architecture, history and flora and fauna, always concerned by the despoliation of natural beauty by industrial greed. He often painted in oils or watercolours and sometimes did pencil drawings whilst travelling.

Against all odds, Jonathan lived to see an exhibition of his own collages and cartoons, shown for six weeks between April and June 2005 at Riverside Studios in Hammersmith. It was his swan-song and a great success.

Prior to this he had for two consecutive years been successful in exhibiting and selling some collages at the Royal Academy's Summer Exhibition.

Two days before he died, when three friends and I were visiting him at Denville Hall, the actors' nursing home, and read to him the comments in the visitors' book from the exhibition, despite his failing speech he had us all laughing as we left.

The next day I mentioned this to him and he commented, 'The adrenalin was good, wasn't it?' He kept his integrity to the end.

He was amazingly brave, kind, very sensitive, exciting, charismatic and brilliantly creative – the love of my life.

Joan Elliott

A retrospective art exhibition at Northampton Museum and Art Gallery (in Jonathan's home town, for which he had much nostalgic affection) is being held from 2nd February to 16th March 2008 in conjunction with the publication of this book.

'1960s cocktail party'